"Sign, Please !"

Larry Liddell

PublishAmerica
Baltimore

© 2011 by Larry Liddell.
All rights reserved. No part of this book may be reproduced, stored in a retrieval system or transmitted in any form or by any means without the prior written permission of the publishers, except by a reviewer who may quote brief passages in a review to be printed in a newspaper, magazine or journal.

First printing

PublishAmerica has allowed this work to remain exactly as the author intended, verbatim, without editorial input.

Hardcover 978-1-4560-3125-1
Softcover 978-1-4560-3126-8
PUBLISHED BY PUBLISHAMERICA, LLLP
www.publishamerica.com
Baltimore

Printed in the United States of America

Dedicated to
Martha and Stephanie
and "The Wild Bunch"
Hayden, Trey, Phoebe, Adam
Amalie, Braxton, Carson, Sawyer

Many thanks to all the celebrities I've met and especially to those who signed their autographs, making this book possible, to Momma and Daddy for not leaving me behind when moving place to place, to Judge Larry Lewis for contributing to the forward to my audio book, to my friends for reading this one and for waiting for the ones in the works, and to my Editor, Diane Donnelly, for the audio book and for her skills, creativity, good humor, and perseverance while helping me bring "Sign, Please!" to my readers.

To Terry,
A great cheerleader for CHS Ole Miss and God! Enjoy!
Amy

Contents

Chapter 1: Heeeerrre's Larry! 9
Chapter 2: Little Partner 12
Chapter 3: Indian Territory 18
Chapter 4: Surprises in Shaw 21
Chapter 5: New York! New York! 26
Chapter 6: Nothing But the Facts 29
Chapter 7: The King and I 32
Chapter 8: REJOICE! 36
Chapter 9: Party Time at Delta State 40
Chapter 10: I Bite the Big Apple 45
Chapter 11: I Aim To Please 52
Chapter 12: Great Seat! Great Show! 54
Chapter 13: P, P and M 58
Chapter 14: Thanks for the Memory 63
Chapter 15: Jack, Be Nimble: PGA MEM 67
Chapter 16: Cash and the Redhead at Ole Miss 69
Chapter 17: That Girl 73
Chapter 18: The Saints Came Marchin' In 78
Chapter 19: I Go To Hollywood 83
Chapter 20: Hollywood Comes to New Orleans 87
Chapter 21: Hello, Dolly 90
Chapter 22: I'm in Love with Reba McEntire 92
Chapter 23: Lonely are the Brave 96
Chapter 24: The Stars Shine for Charity 98
Chapter 25: The Statler Brothers at Miss. State 101
Chapter 26: Truly a True Value 104
Chapter 27: Tiny Bubbles 106
Chapter 28: Oldies 109
Chapter 29: n Goodies 111
Chapter 30: Unsigned Heroes 114
Braggin' Page 117

Chapter 1
"Heeeerrre's Larry!"

I'd like to say it was a dark and stormy night when I popped into the Tri-State Memorial Hospital on June 8, 1942, in Shreveport, Louisiana. I do know, from my birth certificate and subsequent birthdays, that it was at precisely 10:23 PM and that I was the only son of William Walker Liddell and Vina Belle Patman Liddell. Shreveport is home of the "Louisiana Hayride" on KWKH and was to play a big part in my life, a fact I didn't know at the time of my birth.

My dad, an Ole Miss grad, was a pharmacist in Shreveport at the time, but shortly after I was born, he found a better job in Cleveland, Mississippi, at Owens Drug Store, in the small Delta town better known for being the home of Delta State University than for being my hometown. I literally grew up in Cleveland, a great time and place for a kid to grow up, let me tell you.

We lived right across the street from Cleveland High School in a duplex on Bolivar Avenue. I was an adventurous kid and would acquire several "15 minutes of fame," moments of notoriety, and have several infamous experiences on and around Bolivar Avenue. World War II was raging which didn't bother me. Dad made sure of that: I was his "honey bunch," and he provided plenty of love and groceries for our little family.

Mother took care of home and me, making sure I went to school and to church and got a "proper upbringing." She reminded me all too often as I grew about how I "ran her a dog's life," especially during my pre-school days. She said I'd leave the house, and she'd have absolutely no idea where I was, so she'd pray for the town's fire whistle to blow. I was deathly afraid of the siren, a precursor to news reports about the war, with air raid sirens that blasted away, maybe signaling the end of my world.

Whenever I "disappeared," I'd be having a ball. At the end of the school property, I'd join the cotton pickers in the field who would put me inside their cotton sack and "ride" me up and down the endless cotton rows. When the sack got heavy with cotton and was too hard for them to pull, I'd climb out, wave a happy goodbye and be off somewhere else, having a great time looking for more mischief to get into.

From September through May, school buses would line up on Bolivar in front of my house in the afternoons for students to board for their rides home. One of my favorite things to do was to hop on one of the yellow buses and ride the complete route, about an hour and a half run. Then the driver would drop me back in front of the house. Mr. Tedder and Mr. Sanders were my favorite bus drivers. (I wasn't allowed to call them by their first names, so I don't remember them.) They were super nice to me. They'd usually stop at a country store along their route and, depending on the weather, treat me to me a soda

SIGN, PLEASE!

pop, ice cream, popsicle or hot chocolate. As a result of their kindness, my first thought of a good job was to be a bus driver. Not just a school bus driver; I dreamed early on of driving for the Greyhound Bus Lines. As I grew older, I leaned toward driving for Trailways, because their silver and red buses were neater and more colorful than the blue/gray Greyhounds. And their names were cool: Golden Eagles. Silver Eagles. My mother was appalled at the idea idea of my being a bus driver. She was thinking "lawyer, policeman, or fireman," like most kids were thinking. And Mom didn't understand: most of the kids I ran with had their futures planned out for them when they were born. Children of the owner of the seed company, an auto dealer, a preacher, etc., my buddies' destinies were "set."

During one early disappearance, Mother looked out of the front window of the house and spotted me climbing up the outside fire escape of Cleveland High School. I was three at the time, and she was petrified. She didn't yell, for fear I'd fall, and yet she was afraid not to yell!. Suddenly, she saw a window open. Arms reached out, grabbed me and hauled me inside. One of the teachers had spotted my journey. This was the first time I was called down by a teacher and certainly was not to be the last!

We loved music in our home, and I remember in pre-school years that Mother and I would lay on the bed and listen to "The Grand Ole Opry" on our old Zenith radio. My favorite singer was Eddy Arnold, known as "The Old Plowboy." When Eddy was singing, our house was very quiet. My favorite of his songs was, and still is, "I'll Hold You in My Heart." Later in my life, he recorded hits such as, "Make the World Go Away," and "What's He Doing in My World." Even when those tunes were on top of the chart, my favorite was still a little ditty called, "The Last Word in Lonesome is Me."

Chapter 2
"Little Partner"

My life with celebrity began in my pre-school years when my mother discovered movies.

Whether she enjoyed the movies herself or just as entertainment for me, I still benefited.

I don't remember the first movie I ever saw, but for the sake of this tome, I'll make it a Roy Rogers western classic.

Roy became my first hero. And he's still my hero today.

Mother would take me to the movies and stay with me until she could trust me to stay in the theater by myself for the full run on Saturday afternoons. This meant the serial, the cartoon, and the double feature. Mother called it baby-sitting. I called it my first shot at culture!

Roy always wore a white hat, carried two guns, rode a golden Palomino named Trigger, and sang with the Sons of the Pioneers. He had a side-kick named Gabby Hayes. Roy befriended but never kissed a girl, and he always got the bad guys.

SIGN, PLEASE!

And it only took him an hour.

In those days, before tickets went up to a quarter, a dime admission got you into the movie, and for another twenty cents, you could get a bag of popcorn and a Coke! Today, we almost have to float a loan to afford all that!

But I digress....

I had Roy's routine down to a science and loved to "play Roy" when my friends and I were playing cowboys and Indians.

One day, a good-looking 12 year-old girl came to visit her grandmother in the other half of the Bolivar Avenue duplex. Her name was Kay Swayze, and what a beauty she was! I was only six and, even then, had an eye for the girls, having kissed Peggy Sue Montgomery on the first day of first grade.

Kay was too old to be playing cowboys and Indians with me, but she was a great sport, and I was the only boy on the block. I was playing Roy, and she was Dale Evans. My Dad was due to be walking home from work about the time we were looking for the bad guys, so we "galloped" down to the corner on the other side of the high school and hid between two tall bushes, ready to ambush. We'd been there for only a minute when we heard a loud buzzing noise and felt something stinging on our arms and necks.

Yellow jackets!

Kay and I galloped back home as fast as we could, each of us hitting the doors of our respective sides of the duplex, screaming for help! I remember that we were stung multiple times. WOW! My first time to, "take a girl to the bushes." I reckon cowboy Roy had better luck!

One Sunday morning shortly after the yellow jacket attack, my Dad announced that we were going to Memphis to the rodeo! Man, was I excited! I'd never been to a rodeo and, better yet, Roy Rogers was the star of the show! And Trigger was coming! And Dale Evans and Lash LaRue would also be appearing!

We got into our brand new black Studebaker Champion (it had the same name as Gene Autry's horse) and took US Highway 61 to Memphis, 2-lane all the way, passing through the hamlet of Tunica on the route north.

On the right side of the road, there was a café called The Tearoom. We always stopped there for something to eat and drink before going on into Memphis. And on the right side of the road heading south, we always stopped directly across 61 from The Tearoom at The Blue and White on our way back home.

Dad would invariably look at me in Tunica and say with a laugh, "Son, don't ever wind up in Tunica. It's the poorest county in the United States." (There'll be more about Tunica later.)

Dad didn't like to drive in Memphis, so when we arrived in the city, we parked the Studebaker in a parking garage and took a taxi to the Gayoso Hotel. I wasn't sure why Dad booked us into the Gayoso that particular trip and thought maybe it was because it was close to Goldsmith's where Mom liked to shop. I later decided maybe he knew something we didn't.

At the Gayoso, Dad marched me right into the gift shop and sat me down where the magazines were on sale and told me to look through the comic books while he went down to get a haircut. That suited me just fine. I began leafing through the comics until I found the newest Roy Rogers book and began reading.

There's no telling how long I'd been sitting there reading when I felt a tap on my shoulder. I figured it was Dad, back

SIGN, PLEASE!

from his haircut and, reluctant to give up my favorite comic, I just glanced over my shoulder and up.

"What are you looking at, partner?" came the question.

I thought my eyes were playing tricks on me and then thought,"It can't be!"

But it was.

I was staring into the blue eyes of my hero, Roy Rogers!

I was speechless, so he tried tact.

"Do you like that book, partner?" he asked.

All I could do was nod my head.

"Well, let me buy it for you," he smiled, reaching down for my hand. Holding onto the comic, I took his hand, and we walked to the counter together. He left a dime on the counter, and the lady behind the counter just smiled and put my book into a sack.

Roy took the sack with my new comic book and handed it to my Dad who was standing a little behind Roy, smiling proudly.

"Can you spare your son for a few minutes?" Roy asked.

"I guess so," Dad replied, obviously puzzled.

"I'd like to take him up to meet some of my pals," Roy explained, leading me down toward the Gayoso's elevators.

He punched the button, and the elevator door closed, with me holding tight to Roy's hand, never having nerve enough to say a word. When the elevator door opened, we walked down the hall to one of the rooms, and Roy knocked on the door. When it opened, my mouth dropped another inch!

"Larry, I'd like you to meet Dale Evans," he smiled as he removed his white hat.

"Hi, Larry, come on in," she invited me in, to what I came to know as the Presidential Suite. "Where did Roy find you?"

"Reading a comic book," I managed to respond.

"Well, he *can* talk!" Roy laughed. "Where's Lash?"

"Right here," came a voice from the other room.

Looking around, I was staring at one of my Saturday afternoon buddies. Dressed in his black duds but without his hat, there stood Lash LaRue, a non-singing cowboy whose trademark was a whip that hung over his 6-gun. That whip was right where it was supposed to be, and my eyes were as big as saucers as I looked at it.

"Want to touch it?" Lash asked with a smile.

As my head nodded affirmatively, my hand was reaching out and touching the leather whip I'd seen many times in movies at the Ellis Theater in Cleveland.

After everyone gave me their autographs and shook my hand, we all left the suite together, walked back to the elevator and rode together down to the second floor, where Dale and Lash got out. Roy rode down to the lobby with me where Dad was anxiously awaiting my return.

"It's been good meeting you, Partner," Roy said as I stepped out of the elevator.

"Thanks, partner," I smiled and waved back to him as the elevator door was closing.

This was the first and only time I ever met my hero, and I'll never forget him or that great day in Memphis. Roy meant so much to me during his time on earth.

Roy Rogers helped my parents teach me wrong from right, and bad from good. He reinforced what they taught me about what to say and how to respect people, young and old. And I guess, more than anything, he helped me develop a conscience. Roy especially did something for me that persists to this day: he introduced me to the world of celebrity up close. I became hooked on it! And remain hooked to this very day!

SIGN, PLEASE!

After meeting Roy Rogers, Dale Evans, and Lash LaRue, I was focused on obtaining autographs of my favorite entertainers. The more of them I met, the more I realized that they were real people, just as I was...and that they were actually looking forward to meeting people who were their fans. Over the years, my quest for autographs took me to numerous locations where I enjoyed meeting and speaking with many sports and showbiz celebrities.

Chapter 3
"Indian Territory"

At the end of the first grade, my doctor discovered I had a severe asthma condition, one that required expensive treatment that my family could ill afford. Dr. Fitz suggested an alternative plan. He advised Dad to move me to a dry climate, like there was in New Mexico, and said that if we didn't, I'd die.

God love my Dad. He got busy and located a job in Roswell, NM, the very same Roswell that had just been invaded from outer space. Dad went out first and got a place to stay, and my Uncle R. L. Patman drove Mother and me to Roswell. It was the longest trip I'd ever taken, and when we got to New Mexico, I thought I had died and gone to heaven. This wonderful feeling would revisit me again and again over my lifetime, but this was the first time I'd experienced it.

For this Mississippi boy who was a true Roy Rogers fan, Roswell was like heaven! Man, I could play cowboys and Indians with Roy's original cast of characters! There were

SIGN, PLEASE!

more Indians in Roswell than there were African-Americans in Mississippi!

On our block alone, there were a half a dozen or more kids who were Native Americans. And since it was summertime, many of the boys in the neighborhood didn't wear shirts. Wearing only shorts, they looked their part. Of course, I wore my jeans and cowboy shirts, but since cowboy boots hurt my feet, I had to settle for wearing black tennis shoes.

At any rate, I lived the cowboy life in Roswell.

We drove over to Carlsbad Caverns our first week-end out there and went down into this seemingly bottomless pit. We ate lunch down there, and when they turned out the lights, I almost lost my lunch. We were in the blackest black I had ever known! Although this was exciting for a seven year-old boy, I'm not sure I could repeat that adventure today.

A week later, I came home from my daily visit with the Indians and, to my dismay, heard Mother say, "We're moving back to Mississippi."

I was crushed! I really liked this cowboy and Indian style of living. When I protested, Mother just calmly said, "Ask your Daddy about it when he gets home tonight."

When Daddy opened the front door, I was waiting.

"Momma says we're moving back to Mississippi," I said unhappily. "I thought the doctor said I would die if I stayed there."

Dad replied, "Son, our next door neighbor killed a six-foot rattlesnake on his back porch last week-end while we were in Carlsbad. You might die of asthma, but you ain't gonna' die of no rattlesnake bite."

So, that week-end, Uncle R. L. came out and drove Mother and me back back to Shreveport, where I spent every summer of my life until I got out of college. Shreveport was a neat city, and my Aunt Leona Patman Loveless, whom we kids all called Aunt Onie, made it even neater. Suddenly, Dad arrived, and we packed up. He drove us to a little place called Shaw, Mississippi, only 10 miles from Cleveland, in the Mississippi Delta. I was scared I was going to die of asthma the first night we arrived there, but I survived all through second grade.

Chapter 4
"Surprises in Shaw"

The contractor hadn't finished our house in Shaw yet, so until it was ready for occupancy, we moved into a spot above the garage of a guy named Dave "Boo" Ferriss. The name meant nothing to me at the time, although "Boo" Ferriss was to have a gigantic impact on my life.

"Boo" was a Shaw native whose family owned a Gulf service station there. He had been to Mississippi State University on a baseball scholarship and had then signed a major league contract with the Boston Red Sox of the American League.

The season was over for the Red Sox in September, and "Boo" had arrived home. He was outside when I arrived home from school one afternoon, doing some yard work around the Ferriss home.

"Hi, son," he beamed.

"Name's Larry," I replied, shaking his hand.

"People call me 'Boo,'" he replied. "Want to play some catch?"

"Sure," I said, running upstairs to get my glove.

We played catch until I grew tired. It was the first time in my life that I got tired of playing before a grown-up did.

"I enjoyed that," I managed to say at the end of the session.

"So did I," he smiled. "Wait right here."

He disappeared into his house and came out holding a baseball.

"I'd like you to have this," he said, handing me an authentic major league baseball, autographed by every member of the Boston Red Sox — Ted Williams, Dom DiMaggio, all of 'em!

Naturally, I had heard of those guys. I wasn't oblivious about major league baseball. I just didn't know, "Boo."

"Thanks a lot," I exclaimed, running up the stairs to show my prize to Mother.

I've still got that baseball, folks!

That year, I got to be friends in Shaw with Mr. G, the town marshal. Mr. Griffin was a neat guy who walked his rounds in the evening. He wore a gun and a badge, just like the marshals in my Roy Rogers movies, and he also wore cowboy boots. Mr. G would let me walk with him, and sometimes I even rode my bicycle alongside of him. I remember him as a big guy, but he probably wasn't that tall. He sort of reminded me of Hopalong Cassidy (William Boyd).

Many's the night Mr. G and I would jiggle the locks on the front doors of closed businesses in Shaw, just like Matt Dillon and Chester did on "Gunsmoke" years later. When I watch "Gunsmoke" on "TV Land" today, I always think of Mr. Griffin.

One day, after school and before time to make our rounds, Dad phoned me and instructed me in no uncertain terms to get on my bike and hotwheel it down to Germany's Drug

SIGN, PLEASE!

Store where he was a pharmacist. When I arrived, he told Mr. Germany, the store owner, that he'd be right back.

Dad took me across the street to the Hamburger Inn, which I thought odd, since I hadn't asked for anything to eat or drink.

"Do you see anybody you recognize in here?" Dad asked with a smile. Looking over the few customers at that time of day didn't take long, and sure enough, I recognized a man sitting in a booth about midway of the restaurant.

"That looks like Tex Ritter!" I exclaimed.

"It is, son," he replied. "Go see if he'll sign something for you."

I walked back and sidled up to Tex's table and asked shyly, "Mr. Ritter, will you sign a napkin for me?"

"Well," he began, "I suppose I can. Why don't you sit a spell, pal?"

I looked around, but my Dad had slipped out and gone back to the drug store. So I plopped down in the seat across from the singing cowboy.

"What's your name, son?" he asked.

"Larry," I responded with a smile.

"Want a root beer?" he asked, nodding to the waitress. "Are you coming to see the show tonight?"

I didn't even know there was a show, much less if I was going. It was, after all, a school night. However, I wasn't going to let him know it.

"Sure," I shot back quickly, taking a sip of my favorite beverage.

"Do you have a favorite song of mine that you'd like to hear tonight?" he wanted to know.

Well, I sure did, and I wasn't bashful about telling him, either.

"Yep," I told him. "'Rye Whiskey.'"

He threw his head back and laughed loudly.

"Now what do you know about rye whiskey?" Tex roared.

"I know it's a great song of yours," I said seriously.

"That it is, son, that it is, and I'll do it tonight just for you," he told me.

With that, Tex signed the napkin, shook my hand, and gave me the signed souvenir. I went running over to the drug store, waving my new treasure for everybody to see. I then told Dad that we just *had* to go see Tex that night. To my surprise, Dad said he already had the tickets.

That night, Mr. Collier's movie theater was packed as Tex strode onstage, guitar in hand. About midway into the show, Tex paused and asked for the house lights to be turned up.

"This afternoon, I met a young pal of mine at the Hamburger Inn," he began, as the house lights went up. "Is Larry here tonight?"

I yelled, "I'm right here, Tex!" The theater crowd erupted in laughter.

"Well, what was that song you wanted to hear?"

"'Rye Whiskey,'" I yelled back. Again the crowd erupted in laughter.

"Well, this is just for you, son," Tex said, strumming his guitar with the opening chord, and with that, he sang my favorite Tex Ritter song, much to the delight of my Mom and Dad and me.

"Caaaaalll for Philllll-iiipppp Morrr-ray-iss"……. That voice was unmistakable, and we were excited as we made our way to the auditorium of Shaw Elementary School.

SIGN, PLEASE!

Johnny Roventini, the small guy dressed in a bellhop's uniform, was the mascot, for the giant cigarette maker, Phillip Morris. His voice was heard on every Phillip Morris radio commercial. (Remember radio?) Roventini had stopped in Shaw while traveling the South on a personal appearance tour.

As we were entering the auditorium, who should be standing at the door but Johnny himself! Most of the kids didn't recognize him, but I read a lot and had seen his picture in magazine ads for Phillip Morris cigarettes.

"Know who I am?" he asked me. (Why me? I never knew.)

"Yes, you are the Phillip Morris man," I replied with a smile.

"That's right," he seemed surprised. "Do you smoke?"

"No, but my Dad does," I said.

"Here," he said, handing me a sample pack of his brand.

Johnny was then led onto the stage where he was introduced and made a short talk and, finally, cupped his left hand around his mouth, holding a pack in his outstretched right hand, and yelled, "Caalllll forrrr Phil-llip Morr-ray-iss!"as he left the stage.

We kids got in trouble for months after that with the school administration, calling out "Caaallll forrrrrrrr Phil-llip Morr-ray-iss" anytime we felt like it!

Chapter 5
"New York! New York!"

For the next few years after second grade, my life with celebrities took a backseat to school and baseball. We moved to Bossier City LA, to Clarksdale MS, and finally back to Cleveland MS, just in time for fourth grade.

In the Spring of 1954, when I was almost 12, I met country giants Johnny & Jack - Johnny Wright and Jack Anglin — and Kitty Wells and the famous Blackwood Brothers — Edward Reece on piano, first tenor Bobby Ball, baritone James Howell, bass Kemp Higginbotham, and second tenor Cecil Blackwood. All of these stars appeared on the same night at the Wesco Theater in Cleveland. I had been hearing Kitty Wells on the Opry for years.

That same year, my parents took me up north; we drove along Skyline Drive in Virginia to Washington DC. Mother's cousin, U.S. Representative Wright Patman, DEM from TX, showed us the U. S. Capitol. I saw my first major league baseball game: the Washington Senators v the Cleveland

SIGN, PLEASE!

Indians. Bob Porterfield v Mike Garcia! I didn't think it could get any better than that!

We took the train from DC to New York City and saw the Yankees against the Chicago White Sox in Yankee Stadium! And after the game, we went to dinner at Jack Dempsey's Restaurant, where I met the former boxing champion, shook his hand, and got his autograph! It just didn't get any better than that!

I then spent the majority of my young life in Cleveland. Folks there were and still are the best — down-to-earth and friendly. It was then and still is a typical Southern town — the best place in America to grow up, in the best of times — the 50's!

When I turned 13, I got a job selling records at the Melody Record Corner, owned and operated by Lawrence "Fedu" Feduccia. Melody Record Corner, known as "The Corner," was one of the most popular and well-known landmarks in downtown Cleveland, located on the corner of Sharpe and Sunflower (now University). It had a soda fountain and a jukebox — and you could preview any song on a 45 rpm disc to see if you wanted to buy it or not. The store carried everything from jazz to opera and was one of the best-stocked music stores in the Delta, and one of the busiest. Sunflower led directly to Delta State College and was well-traveled — it was a popular neighborhood. I remember selling B. B. King and Bo Diddley records there before I even began to like their music.

Fedu was an entrepreneur who knew how to make a buck and didn't mind paying his help a living wage — or at least a livable allowance! He also managed WCLD Radio. In an effort to boost listenership, he ran a contest to find a boy and girl to co-host a radio show one night a week. The night in jeopardy was Wednesday, customarily "prayer meeting night" in the mostly Protestant community of Cleveland. Fedu insisted that I enter the contest, and, much to my surprise, I was the boy selected by "an independent committee of judges." The girl selected was Juliet Kossman, a young lady who was the daughter of the owner of Kossman Motors, one of the station's largest advertisers. The judges had, of course, picked the two best contestants and we were, of course, grateful for that.

Radio was the start of my brief career in show business. Fortunately, Juliet had her own Buick and picked me up for the ride to the station every Wednesday night, since I was still too young to get a driver's license. Our show was a hit, and listenership did pick up on Wednesday nights. When the school year ended, Juliet went off to college, and I was hired by the station to host a week-end show.

Chapter 6
"Nothing But the Facts"

In the summer of 1955, I encountered another of my lifetime heroes — Jack Webb, the star of "Dragnet," my all-time favorite television and radio shows.

Jack came to Shreveport on August 2nd that summer as part of the promotional tour for his movie, "Pete Kelly's Blues." The movie told the story of a 1920's trumpet player who led a harrowing life, filled with mobsters, women and booze. Peggy Lee, a fine sultry-voiced singer and actress, won an Academy Award for her role as a mobster's singing girlfriend in the movie.

My Aunt Onie drove me to the airport to witness Jack's arrival and left me with the instruction to, "Find your own way home."

When his plane, named "The Pete Kelly Special," arrived, Jack was the first one to step through the door and walk down the ramp. I immediately ran to the front of the airport and spotted the waiting limousine. As Jack got into the limo and closed the door, I stuck my autograph book through the window, but he rolled up the window. It caught my hand, and the driver had no clue I was being dragged along at 20 mph as the limo began to pull away. Jack told the driver, "Whoa," and smiled and rolled down the window, saying, "Sorry, son, no autographs."

I was, of course, disappointed...but not discouraged.

That night, I was the first in line at the Strand Theater for the Shreveport premiere of the movie, after which Jack was to appear. After the movie, which I thoroughly enjoyed, I went out the side Exit of the theater and made my way back behind the theater to where Jack's limo was waiting. The only trouble now was that it was raining like hell, lightning was flashing and thunder was crashing. I couldn't afford to get my autograph book wet, so I kept it under my rain jacket and waited until Jack made a dash for the limo.

He recognized me - or maybe it was my arm - and smiled, helped his wife into the limo and turned to me and said, "You'd better get under the overhang, young man, or you're going to drown." And with that, Jack got into his limo which sped off in the direction of the old Washington-Youree Hotel where he and his entourage were staying.

Soaked to the skin and now discouraged in addition to being disappointed, I caught a trolley and went to my Uncle R. L.'s house to spend the night. The Jack Webb experience marked the first time in my life that I had missed getting an autograph when the opportunity presented itself. However, it wouldn't be the only time.

Four years later, when I was 16, we were living back in Clarksdale where Dad was a pharmacist at Palace Drugs. Robert Mitchum was in Oxford shooting, "Home from the Hill," which proved to be one of his most powerful

SIGN, PLEASE!

performances. I drove over to Oxford to see if I could get any autographs.

Sure enough, I found the movie set, an old home right off the famous town square. I watched as they shot a scene and waited for my chance. I didn't have to wait long, as the director yelled, "Cut! Wrap!" When he heard the word, "Wrap," Mitchum immediately headed for his trailer which was parked just down the street and around the corner from the set.

I followed, with my trusty autograph book and pen in hand.

"Mr. Mitchum," I said, catching up to him as he neared his trailer, "may I have your autograph, please?"

Barely taking time to look over his shoulder, he reached for the door of his trailer and retorted in a most dramatic fashion, "Write for it, son!" And with that, the star opened his trailer door, entered, and slammed the door behind him! Maybe he was having a bad day. I never knew. All I knew was that it was the second time I was refused an autograph when I was up close and had the chance to get one.

There have been many times when I was in close proximity to a celebrity and didn't ask for an autograph. There are times when you just can't do that, and I've regretted missing out on those occasions, but I've always felt I did the right thing by not asking just then.

Toward the end of the eventful year of 1955, Uncle R. L. was hospitalized, suffering from two broken vertebrae. R. L. had been a passenger in a car driven by his buddy Mac who lost control of the car in some loose gravel. The car flipped several times, landing bottom-side up on the side of the road. Thankfully, both Mac and my uncle survived, and Uncle R.L.'s back healed without complication after their spectacular crash.

Chapter 7
"The King and I"

I took a vacation in November of 1955 and went to visit Aunt Onie and Uncle Flake in Shreveport, home of the popular Louisiana Hayride show. It was second-only to the Grand Ole Opry among country fans. In 1955, "country" definitely was not "my thing." I was addicted to baseball, rock and roll, and "Dragnet," and in that order.

My cousin Billy Ray Patman was also visiting, and he was a country music fan wanting to go to The Hayride. I didn't want to go and said I wanted to go instead to see the Shreveport Sports play baseball in a Texas League game on Sunday. Ever the diplomat, Aunt Onie negotiated a deal in which I would accompany Billy Ray to The Hayride Saturday night, and he'd go to the ball game with me on Sunday. Onie called is a compromise. I called it blackmail, but it was that or no ball game at all. So off we went on Saturday night to The Hayride.

Needless to say, I was bored stiff. The fiddles and steel guitars were driving me crazy, to say nothing of the performers.

SIGN, PLEASE!

So I kinda' drifted off to sleep as the program went on…and on…and on. Suddenly, I was awakened by loud screams and catcalls. When my eyes were drawn to the stage, I saw this guy shaking his hips and gyrating like crazy. I thought he was having some sort of seizure while he was still on his feet.

"What's happening?" I asked Billy Ray, who was rocking with the crowd.

"That's Elvis Presley from Memphis," he explained.

I had never heard of Elvis except for selling some of his records on Sun label at The Corner, no more sales than I'd made of Johnny Cash and Jerry lee Lewis' records, also on Sun. I was quick to notice, however, that Elvis had something. I was too young to know anything about sex appeal, but I knew he was going places, and I didn't mean the Grand Ole Opry. This guy was SOME big!

I got up to leave, and Billy Ray said, "Where are you going?"

"Backstage," I shot back. "I'm going to get his autograph."

"You can't get back there," he protested, following me.

"Just follow me and keep your mouth shut," I yelled over the screams of every female in the Shreveport Municipal Auditorium.

We just walked right past the guard who was caught up in the excitement of the moment like everyone else there. The police had already formed a human chain in front of the stage to hold the crowd back.

When Elvis finished, he walked offstage to where we were standing. I had already grabbed a piece of paper off a desk, along with a pencil.

"Can I have your autograph?" I asked pleasantly.

"Sure," he smiled, grabbing the paper and pencil.

He signed it, "Thanks, Elvis Presley," and handed it back to me.

"Where are you from?" he asked casually.

"Cleveland, Mississippi," I answered proudly.

"Mississippi," he exclaimed. "I'm from Tupelo. Girls, move over! Let this boy sit down!"

There were half a dozen girls with official backstage passes sitting in theater seats provided for them. Elvis forced them to move, and he and I sat down and talked for fifteen minutes about Tupelo and Cleveland. During our conversation, I mentioned that I sold records at The Melody Record Corner and that I had my own radio show on WCLD in Cleveland. It was wild! When I shook his hand in parting, little did I know that this was the beginning of a relationship that would last for the next 22 years.

Months later, I was hosting my radio show when the phone rang. It wasn't unusual for the phone to ring during the show, since I routinely took requests. But this was the most unique phone call I ever took.

"Larry, this is Elvis," said the voice.

"Yeah, right," I replied, instantly thinking it was my cousin.

"No, seriously, this is Elvis. Remember? From The Hayride?" he said with a laugh.

"You're kidding, right?" was my only reply. I had no clue as to how to patch him through to the live show or even to tape him. And what were the chances that the station engineer, Pete Webb, would believe it was actually Elvis Presley on the phone?

So I just talked with The King. He had just released his second million-seller single, "Hound Dog," which was on the A side. I like the B side better, a little thing called, "Don't Be Cruel."

"I can barely hear you on my radio," Elvis laughed. I was surprised he could hear me at all, as Memphis is 100 miles from Cleveland, and WCLD was only a 5,000 watt station.

"Can you play, 'Don't Be Cruel,' for me?" he asked.

"Sure," I said.

As we were hanging up, I heard Elvis say, "Thank you very much."

Shortly after my week-end show debuted, Fedu left the radio station and built the city's second station which he wanted to call WDSC to reflect Delta State College. There was already a station with those call letters, so the FCC assigned the call letters of WDSK to the new station, assigning it 1410 am. I'm proud to say that I was to be the third hired employee of WDSK and that my week-end gig proved as exciting and rewarding as my Wednesday night gig.

Chapter 8
"REJOICE!"

In 1957, I got my driver's license. My driver ed teacher, Coach Gene Meadows, taught me just about everything I know about driving, and coach's instructions have saved my life more than a few times. So now that I could drive myself, on my visits to Shreveport I often drove across the bridge over the Red River into Bossier City, home of "The Bossier Strip." The Strip was a row of night clubs along US 80. Tall for my age, I was never "carded" as I entered joints on the strip, places forbidden to anyone under 21.

One night at the old Stork Club, a really funny comedian named Brother Dave Gardner was the headliner in the main showroom. It was the first time I'd heard of him, and that evening was the beginning of a long friendship.

I enjoyed Brother Dave's show a lot and, much to my surprise, saw him at the bar afterwards. I struck up a conversation and went back to see him perform again and again. He was a real funny guy both on and off stage. He wrote

SIGN, PLEASE!

in my autograph book, "Rejoice! Brother Dave." "Rejoice" was Brother Dave's way of (1) putting an exclamation point in one of his stories and/or (2) bridging the gap between one story and another.

In 1960, Elvis staged his first concert in Memphis after his return from the Army. It was also his first Memphis show since buying Graceland. Somehow, I managed to get tickets to the show. My girlfriend Cissy Haley and I drove up from Clarksdale where my family had been living since '58. It was quite a show. George Jessel was Master of Ceremonies. Featured stars were Floyd Cramer, best known for his hit, "Last Date," The Jordanaires, and, yes, REJOICE! Brother Dave Gardner.

After the show, "Elvis Has Left The Building," was announced. Nevertheless, I grabbed Cissy's hand and led her to the tunnel that led backstage.

"What are we doing back here?" Cissy asked breathlessly.

"Just a minute," I smiled confidently.

And sure enough, a minute later, out walked Brother Dave and his wife.

Spotting me, he broke into a wide grin, saying, "Hey brother, what are you doing back here?"

I introduced Cissy, and he introduced his wife. Cramer strode by, as did Jessel, but we were locked in conversation with Brother Dave. We told our ladies of our friendship and brought each other up to date on our activities since our last meeting. My Dad had died in '59, and I had received an athletic scholarship for track which would cover half of my expenses at Delta State.

Brother Dave asked innocently, "Are y'all coming out to Grease-Land?" intentionally mispronouncing the name of Elvis' new home.

"No, Dave," I laughed, "our invitation must have gotten lost in the mail."

"Well, you don't need one," he laughed, "just tell 'em Brother Dave sent you."

"Yeah, right," I laughed as we parted.

As we got into the car and I shifted gears, Cissy screamed as loudly as she could, scaring me into slamming on the brakes!

"What's wrong?" I asked hastily.

"Oh, nothing," she smiled innocently. "I just love the way you shift gears with your wrist. You move your wrist just like Elvis."

Hitting US 61 heading back home, Cissy screamed again. "This isn't the way to Graceland."

"We can't go there," I assured her. "Brother Dave was just being nice."

Although I didn't know it, the invitation that Brother Dave had extended was good. He even mentioned to Elvis that I would probably be coming by, because he knew we were also friends.

See, back in '57, a couple of years before the Memphis concert, I'd been in Memphis to see Dewey Phillips, a DJ at WHBQ. Phillips had been the first DJ to play an Elvis song on the radio. WHBQ was located in the Hotel Chisca. While I was there to see Dewey, Elvis came in via the fire escape in the alley behind the hotel. I casually mentioned my fun times with Brother Dave. Elvis laughed and said he, too, knew Brother Dave, and he thought a lot of him, too.

Elvis and I chatted for about an hour up in the studio. Then we went down for hamburgers and milk shakes at the Krystal around the corner from the Chisca and just had a good old boys' night out. It was cool.

SIGN, PLEASE!

When I next saw Elvis in '72, he asked me why I'd never showed up at Graceland that night 12 years earlier. His mind was a sharp as it had ever been. When I told him I didn't think we could've gotten in, he chastised me greatly, saying he had personally called his Uncle Vester at the gate and left implicit instructions to let Cissy and me in!

Elvis and I never corresponded by mail and were together in person only four times in our lives. However, when we were together or on the phone, it was like we were family.

I will always regret not accepting Brother Dave's invitation to Graceland following that 1960 concert.

My relationship with El was special to me, and I like to think it was special to him as well. It was the night I visited with Dewey Phillips in '56 that I realized how special it was, when El walked in and remembered me from our first visit in Shreveport in '55.

I visited with Elvis in Seattle in '76, 10 months before his untimely death. He was always the same. He never changed.

Chapter 9
"Party Time at Delta State"

College was a four-year party-for me. I was Sports Information Director at Delta State, thanks to Boo Ferris, the DSC Athletic Director. I never missed a sporting event on campus and attended many off-campus events as well, I was also Sports Editor of the school newspaper, *The Miss Delta* (now, *The Statement*). And my senior year, I was honored to be elected Editor of the paper.

I had served as interim Sports Editor at the Clarksdale Press Register during the summer following my graduation from Clarksdale High. Unbeknownst to me, Boo had read my stuff, remembered me from those days in Shaw, and came to the Press Register offices to recruit me.

All the sports news at Delta State went from me to Lee Baker, Sports Editor of the *Jackson Daily News*, to Wayne Thompson, Sports Editor of the *Jackson Clarion Ledger*, to the Jack Bigbees, Senior and Junior, Sports Editor and Sports Columnist, respectively, of the *Memphis Press Scimitar*, and

SIGN, PLEASE!

David Bloom, Sports Editor of the *Memphis Commercial Appeal*. J was happy that they all later recommended me to the folks at Ole Miss and at the New Orleans Saints.

I was also able to meet several music groups who visited the Delta State campus and some who came within driving distance of Cleveland. The first of these was The Brothers Four who signed my book, "To Larry, our very best wishes, Bob, John, Dick, and Mike."

It had rained all day, and the Walter Sillers Coliseum on campus was finished, but the parking lot was not. There was mud everywhere. As a freshman, I was appointed valet to the singers which, simply put, meant that whatever they wanted, I was to provide. Period. No questions asked.

The Brothers Four pulled up in their limo, and before I could warn them, John opened the door and jumped out, right into the mud. His shoes were covered. The other three escaped having their shoes baptized by asking the driver to get a little closer to the curb.

I got busy shining John's shoes and had them presentable by showtime. While I was shining the shoes, I provided the group with local and campus tidbits they could use during the show. One item brought the house down.

One of our campus security guards was known to students as "The Shadow." He prowled around the campus late at night, presenting a shadowy silhouette. At the time, there was a famous radio program called, "The Shadow" with a well-known introduction. I told the band about this guy, and they asked me to point him out during the show.

Well, as it happened, the security guard in question walked right in front of the stage while the guys were in between songs. I gave John the high sign from my vantage point backstage, and he began: "Who knows what danger lurks behind the squeaking door?" (just as the spotlight hit the security guard). "THE SHADOW KNOWS I" Every student in the audience and I suspect some of the faculty rose to their feet in thunderous laughter.

After the show, The Brothers thanked me for everything I had done for them. As they got into the limo for their ride back to the Memphis Airport, John stuck his head out the window and smiled, "Hey, Larry!" Thinking there must be something else they needed, I responded, "Yes, John." "Watch the mud!" he laughed as the limo pulled away.

Another group that appeared at DSC during my years there was The Four Preps who brought me to my feet with their version of "26 Miles." They signed my book, "To Larry, Four Preps, Glen, Bruce, Marvin and Ed." When I visited Catalina Island years later, my mind flashed back to the night when this group sang "26 Miles" at their 1961 concert in Mississippi.

In '64, The Limeliters made a Coke commercial, and I loved it. So when they came to Memphis, I took my autograph book and returned to Ellis Auditorium, where Elvis had performed four years earlier. The group sang the song featured in the commercial, "There's a Meeting Here Tonight," but failed to sing "Hey Li Le Li Le," a song which included audience participation. After the show, I went backstage and chastised them for not singing that song.

"The audience was not receptive to our music," spokesperson Lou Gottllieb responded candidly. "They were not into the concert enough to inspire us to think they were inspired enough to think up the two-line couplets necessary to make the whole thing work."

That mouthful was Lou's way of saying, "It was a lousy audience."

SIGN, PLEASE!

While getting the Limeliters to sign my book (Lou Gottlieb, Glen Yarborough and Alex Hassiley) they casually mentioned they were booked into Jackson MS later in the Spring. I hustled back to Cleveland, called a few friends and arranged for tickets. Several weeks later, my roommate Steve LaMastus and I rode down to the capital city to catch their show. I was armed with a two-line couplet, just in case the audience was "into" the concert.

I met the guys in the band as they drove up in their rental cars. Lou was driving, and Alex was his passenger. Noticing me open his door, Alex exclaimed, "Hey, Lou. Guess who's here?"

"Who?" Lou asked.

"Larry from Memphis," he laughed, extending his hand.

"Where's Glen?" I asked, as he wasn't in the car.

"We don't let him ride with us," Lou shot back. "Here he comes now."

Rounding the corner was a Volkswagen (I didn't know you could rent 'em) with his beloved bass fiddle tied on top!

"Now you see why we don't let him ride with us," Alex exclaimed.

Upon entering the antiquated Jackson Municipal Auditorium, Lou stopped us cold, saying dramatically, "Guys, do you know where we are?"

"No, Lou, where are we?" Alex played along.

"This is where Grant said, 'War is hell!'" Lou informed us.

Toward the end of the Limeliters' show, Lou asked for the house lights to be brought up and introduced, "Hey Li Le Li Le," inviting the audience to provide "two-line couplets for our listening pleasure."

Finally, he noticed my hand waving frantically. I was the last person chosen.

"Well, it looks like Larry might have something to contribute to our frivolity tonight," he said enthusiastically. "OK, Larry, let's hear it."

Suddenly, the house lights went out, and a spotlight was shining only on me. Bravely I stood and in perfect pitch (right, Roomie?), bellowed out: "Barnett came for the pot of gold. Hey Li Le Li. Now he's got it, I've been told. Hey Li Le Li Le Lo."

Well, the audience roared its approval and gave me a standing ovation for my effort. Lou, one of the most educated men in show business, knew that Mississippi GovernoR Ross Barnett had recently installed gold fixtures in all the baths of the governor's mansion.

"Ah, yes, political satire," Lou boomed over the ovation. "I might have known."

You had ta' be there!

Chapter 10
"I Bite the Big Apple"

As editor of the college newspaper, it was my responsibility to keep the college population apprised as to what was going on around the campus. I was on top of most everything involving campus life.

The Student Government Association scheduled a spring concert featuring The Journeymen. Three weeks prior to the concert, Robert Simonton, college information director and faculty advisor to The Miss Delta, called me in and informed me that the paper had won a First Place Award for Typography from the Columbia University Scholastic Press Association, and that college President, James M. Ewing, had authorized me to fly to New York City for the award ceremony.

Now, Dr. Ewing and I were on opposite sides of most issues, and it was totally out of character for him to send me anywhere, much less to New York, at college expense. However, Simonton insisted that I not question this, just take the trip and have a good time. This was one of the greatest trips I have ever taken in my life.

We picked up a tailwind, and the American Airlines jet was an hour ahead of our scheduled ETA in New York. The sound system sprang to life. "Ladies and gentlemen, this is the Captain speaking. We are descending so that you might see a little of Washington, DC, our nation's capitol. As we break cloud cover, off the left wing of the aircraft you will be able to see the Washington Monument and in the distance, the US Capitol Building. Off the right wing, you will be able to see Arlington National Cemetery, final resting place of President John Fitzgerald Kennedy. We will be arriving in New York on schedule."

And as we were descending to land at LaGuardia, the Captain returned to the mic: "Ladies and gentlemen, off the left wing of the aircraft, you should be able to see clearly the Statue of Liberty, a gift to America from France. If you are not able to see the Statue of Liberty as we break cloud cover, we are in a hell of a lot of trouble." Fortunately, the lady was there and we landed safely.

It might have just looked the same, but my hotel, The Bristol, reminded me a lot of the hotel where my family and I had stayed in '54; it was called The Hotel Henry at that time. I was in the heart of the theater district at 123 West 44th Street, just off Broadway. When I arrived, I made a dash for the St. James theater where "Hello, Dolly" had just opened. I asked at the ticket window for a ticket to the Saturday performance.

"Which month?" the ticket seller asked solemnly.

"Month?" I shot back incredulously. "I'm talking about *this* Saturday."

"Young man," she smiles, "we are sold out until the middle of July."

SIGN, PLEASE!

"Look, M'am," I shot back, "I'm only here until Sunday, and I may never get back here,

and I just want to see a Broadway play, and I am told this is the one to see. Isn't there some way I can get in?"

Maybe it was my southern drawl. Maybe it was my Delta State blazer that caught her eye. She excused herself and left the booth. Moments later, she returned with what she called a "Patron's Ticket."

"How much is a Patron's Ticket," I asked.

"Fifty dollars," she replied.

Swallowing hard, I shelled out two twenties and a ten spot.

"Enjoy," she said with a smile.

"Thanks," I replied, walking away happy, on my way to see my first Cinerama movie, "It's a Mad, Mad, Mad, Mad World," on Broadway at the Warner Brothers Cinerama.

The next morning, I strolled down to the NBC studios and stood outside the NBC windows, waving with the rest of the Today Show fans. As the cameras flicked off, I ran inside and stood by the studio door. When the door opened, out walked Jack Lescoulie the sports and weather guy, with Frank Blair the news guy. I shook hands with them while waiting for Hugh Downs, the show's host.

When Downs came out, he was walking fast toward the elevator. I stuck my notebook in his hand and wrote, while walking, Hugh Downs. It was then that he noticed my Delta State blazer and asked suddenly, "Where is Delta State?"

"In the Mississippi Delta, about 100 miles south of Memphis," I replied.

"How far from Ole Miss," he asked, punching the elevator button.

"About 70 miles," I said.

47

The elevator door opened, and he ushered me in while asking, "What was the feeling at Delta State during the riot?"

Well, I knew I was being interviewed ever so slyly by a network news professional.

Carefully choosing my words, I replied that as editor of the school paper, we had an open line to the Ole Miss newspaper, *The Daily Mississippian*, and had stayed up all night getting minute-by-minute updates. By this time, we were in Downs' private office having coffee. We chatted for another 15 minutes, and he got up and asked, "Is there anything else I can do for you while you are in New York?" Funny he should ask.

My favorite TV shows at the time were on NBC: "That Was The Week That Was" (TW3) and "The Tonight Show with Jack Paar." So I told Hugh Downs that I would like to get tickets for those two shows for Friday. "Well, there's a problem, he smiled. "The Tonight Show is taped at the same time TW3 is on live. Let me see what I can do."

Downs picked up the phone, dialed an extension, said something, and then told me to wait in his office for the page. He said he had a meeting to go to, shook my hand, and left me in his private office. Yes, I did sit in his chair for a short time — like a minute.

Momentarily, the page came in and asked if I were Larry Liddell. Confirming that I was indeed, the page handed me an envelope, saying, "There's a blue ticket for The Tonight Show and a white ticket for TW3 in the envelope."

"What does that mean?" I inquired.

"Well," he said, "a blue ticket guarantees you a seat, while a white ticket puts you on standby. Be sure to be in line by 4 p.m. or you will miss either show."

We rode down in the elevator together, and I went out to Columbia University for the first of two days of conferences,

SIGN, PLEASE!

during one of which I had a tete-s-tete with famed columnist David Susskind. During his presentation, Susskind had put down the great State of Mississippi at a "racist nation."

I asked him, "Have you ever been to Mississippi?"

"No," he admitted.

"Well, before condemning the great state of Mississippi, I'd suggest you come down and meet some of the people who live there and learn a little about them before branding them as 'racists'."

After the session, Susskind came up to me and apologized for, as he so aptly put it, "lumping all the citizens into one barrel of bad apples."

Needless to say, this was one incident where I didn't think it appropriate to ask for an autograph.

Friday afternoon at 4 p.m., I was in line at NBC, envelope in hand. I had gotten into The Tonight Show line, figuring I had no chance to get a blue ticket for TW3.

"Mr. Liddell. Mr. Larry Liddell." I heard a voice paging me.

"Here I am," I identified myself.

"Come with me," he ordered.

"Wait a minute, pal," I hesitated. "I'm seventh in line here which puts me on the front row. I ain't leaving it to go anywhere."

"Trust me, Mr. Liddell," he said. I must have looked older than my 21 years. "Come with me."

Reluctantly, I followed him about 15 yards to someone I learned was the head page. He sat majestically on a raised platform in the lobby.

"Do you have any envelope with you?" he asked.

"Yes, I do," I replied testily.

"Give it to me," he ordered.

"Whoa," I said quickly. "First, I am jerked out of line, and now you are going to take away my tickets? Why? What rule have I broken?"

"Just give me the envelope, please," he ordered again.

Feeling like I had no choice, I handed him my prize possession of the moment — the envelope given to me by the page at the instruction of Hugh Downs.

Taking my envelope, the head page handed me another envelope, this one bearing the return address: Hugh Downs, NBC's Today Show.

Not leaving my position, I opened the envelope to find a blue ticket to TW3 with a handwritten note that said simply, "Enjoy!"

Meekly, I looked up at the head page and asked, "Where is the line for TW3?"

"I'll escort you there, if you will follow me," the page who had jerked me out of the Tonight Show line replied as he took me by the arm. He walked me right up to the front of the line and whispered something to the page there; he immediately placed me in front of the line. This caused some grumbling among those who had been standing in line for no telling how long.

Presently, the doors opened, and we were led into the studio where, sure enough, I was on the front row, far to stage right. I thoroughly enjoyed the show, so much so that upon my return to campus the following Monday, a classmate asked me, "Were you in the audience Friday night at TW3? I could swear I heard you laugh!" I did and still do have a signature laugh that's quite unmistakable! The skit that caused my outburst during the show involved a prisoner who pleads guilty to public drunkenness and is brought before a Dallas judge who exclaims, "30 days in the Dallas County jail."

SIGN, PLEASE!

"Oh, no," the prisoner pleads, dropping to his knees, "anything but there, Judge. I'll never get out alive."

(You may remember that this was less than four months after the assassination of Lee Harvey Oswald by Jack Ruby in the basement of the Dallas County Jail.)

After the show, since I was the first one in, I was the last one out of the studio. As the page was way up front, he had no chance to see me dash inside a door that plainly said, "No Admittance Stage Entrance."

Once behind the door, I found myself in a myriad of hallways. Not knowing exactly which way to go, I pointed myself in the direction I thought was the stage I had just come from. I came to a T in the hall. Which way to go? Suddenly a door opened, and out walked Jack Paar who had just finished taping The Tonight Show.

"Can I help you, young man?" he asked seriously.

"I'm looking for the TW3 stage," I answered confidently so as not to give away the fact that I was trespassing.

"Right through that door," he courteously pointed to my right.

"Thank you, sir," I responded. I did so want to ask him for his autograph and knew it would tip him off that I was not supposed to be there. So I didn't. I have always regretted that.

As Jack Paar walked away in his Charlie Chaplin walk, I heard him say, "Lost at NBC; imagine that! Heh, heh, heh."

Chapter 11
"I Aim To Please"

I opened the door Jack Paar had indicated, and sure enough, I was on the stage, and the cast of TW3 was just milling around, chatting. Trying to be as inconspicuous as possible, I drifted over to Henry Morgan and asked him to sign my book. While signing, he asked where Delta State was located.

"In Mississippi," I answered, knowing what the response would be. But I was wrong.

"Mississippi?" He yelled out. "Hey, Roscoe, come over here. This guy wants to talk to you." Roscoe Lee Brown was an African-American actor on the show.

"Roscoe, this guy is from Mississippi," Morgan informed his friend.

"Don't hit me no mo', boss, please, don't hit me no mo'," Brown picked up the bit, kneeling on the stage. "I promise to work harder, boss, just don't hit me no mo'!"

I was petrified. Not only did they now know I didn't belong, they were creating a scene that caused everybody on the set

SIGN, PLEASE!

to take notice! I was dead meat. Looking for a place to run, I just stood there in shear fright! Laughing, Henry put his arm around me and asked me my name. Telling him, he said to everyone, "It's alright. Larry is just wanting some autographs, and I thought we'd have a little fun." With that explanation, I became a pseudo cast member. The musical director (Dick Noel) came over and signed my book as did Sandy Baron, Mike Robert, and, of course, Brown, who signed: "Thank you, Roscoe Lee Brown."

Then I was facing the beautiful Nancy Ames, who signed, "To Larry, Best Wishes Always, Nancy Ames." I was weak in the knees as I began to walk away after thanking them for making this a most memorable night. But it got better. As I was walking away, Nancy asked, "Say, what are you doing tonight?"

Turning around, I asked, "Are you asking me?"

"Yes," she smiled. "I'm having some friends over, and I'd love for you to be my guest."

"Nothing," I almost yelled too loudly.

Nancy gave me her address, and I walked away, almost floating. In the hallway outside the studio, I ran into Chad Mitchell of The Chad Mitchell Trio, the group which had been the musical guest on the show. Chad was most gracious in signing my autograph book, as were Joe Frasier and Mike Kobluck.

I went back to my hotel, changed into more comfortable clothes, and after an hour or so, took a taxi over to the address Nancy had provided. When I buzzed the apartment number, her voice responded, "Come on up!" There, I spent the next three hours talking, much to the delight of everyone who had never heard a southern accent before! They poured me into a taxi about midnight to go back to my hotel. It was quite a night, what I remember of it!

Chapter 12
"Great Seat! Great Show!"

The next day during ceremonies at the Waldorf Astoria, I accepted *Miss Delta*'s national typography award. This was quite an honor for staff and a paper from the Mississippi Delta, I'll tell you. The grand ballroom was filled with student journalists from all over the country, and there I was on stage accepting a first place plaque. Walking out, I noticed that comedian Jack Carter was appearing in the Empire Room, the Waldorf's showroom. Casually, I asked if there was room for one more.

"Dinner show or cocktail show?" the lady asked. I didn't know one from the other.

"Whichever show I can see after I see, "Hello, Dolly," was my reply.

"You've got tickets to 'Dolly?'" she looked up.

"Well, I've got one, and that's all I need," I shot back quickly.

SIGN, PLEASE!

"Would you like a limo to pick you up at the theater," she wanted to know. I looked around to make sure she was talking to me.

"The reason I asked: you could probably make the cocktail show, if you have a limo waiting," she explained.

"What would a limo cost?" I asked, realizing I was getting low on funds.

"It's complimentary, courtesy of the hotel," she was beginning to get exasperated.

"Well, fine, yes, sure," I stammered.

After watching Carol Channing charm her audience at the St. James Theater, I emerged to find a number of black limos parked outside the theater. Looking around, I spotted a driver holding up a sign that read: "Liddell." The limo ride was wonderful! I felt like a celebrity!

I found that my table for Jack Carter was front and center. It was a miracle. I sat and ordered a drink and relaxed as I watched the room begin to fill up. A guy came over to my table, and I recognized him from seeing him on TV. It was Jack Carter himself.

"Hi. I'm Jack Carter," he extended his hand.

"I'm Larry Liddell," I stood and shook his hand. I saw him looking at my school blazer. "Delta State is in the Mississippi Delta, 100 miles south of Memphis."

"Well, shut my mouth," he put on his best southern drawl. "I think I have found myself a true southern gentleman." We chatted a few more minutes, then he got up, smiled and said, "See you later."

The lights dimmed as a voice intoned, "Ladies and gentlemen, the Empire Room is pleased to present, live and in person, Jack Carter!"

His opening line was, "Damn, it's good to know that I'm live and in person. I was beginning to think I was dead and invisible." There wasn't a serious moment in the show until about midway through, he asked for the house lights to be brought up and directed the spotlight to my table.

"Ladies and gentlemen, I want you to meet a true southern gentleman," he said, hopping down off the stage and handing me the microphone. "Just talk, Larry, just talk about anything you want to tell the fine folks here tonight." I told them who I was and where I was from and explained a little about what I was doing in New York. The audience howled. You would have thought it was the first time they had actually heard a person with a southern accent talk!

Finally, Jack took the mic back with a short, "Give me the mic back, you're getting bigger laughs than me!"

After the show, as I was about to pay my tab and leave, Jack came running over and told the waiter, "Put his tab on my bill, pal. Larry, I want you to meet some friends of mine." He grabbed me by the arm and led me over to another table filled with people.

"Larry, I want you to meet my friend, Jule Styne," he said. The name meant nothing to me at the time, but Jack told me that Styne was in the songwriters' hall of fame and wrote, "If I Give My Love to You," among other hit songs.

Carter then introduced me to his wife, and then to the next guy at the table, a man named Richard Rogers, "of the team of Rogers and Hammerstein." Now, I *had* heard of *them*.

Before I left, I had all of their autographs and memories that will last a lifetime.

Remember, college classes had been a sideline of mine for four years. That summer, while taking driver's ed in order to graduate, I ventured to the Miss Mississippi Pageant,

SIGN, PLEASE!

following Colleen Kinney, the reigning Miss Delta. While there, I met Miss Louisiana and Miss George, both of whom signed my autograph book with personal notes. Linda Baucum, Miss Louisiana '64 wrote: "Larry, Best wishes always to a Shreveport guy, Linda Baucum," while Nancy Middleton wrote: "To Larry, Sincere Wishes, Nancy Middleton, Miss Georgia '64." I wonder where they are today and, wherever they are, I thank them for signing my book.

Chapter 13
"P, P and M"

After graduating from DSC, I returned to Clarksdale as the full-time Sports Editor for the *Press Register*. The paper had a small staff, so all staff members volunteered for different tasks. City Editor Bill Skelton knew he could count on me to cover local as well as nearby entertainment events, so I became infamous for volunteering for the unofficial role of "entertainment director."

One of the first assignments he sent me on was to see Mary Martin in "Peter Pan." It was a masterpiece and, yes, I went backstage yet again at Ellis Auditorium in Memphis. I got Mary Martin's autograph. Not only was she an outstanding singer and actress, she was a delightful woman.

One of the highlights of my stint as entertainment writer for the paper was my coverage of the Peter, Paul and Mary Concert at the Ellis on April 2, 1965. While arranging for my press credentials, I asked permission to interview the somewhat controversial trio.

SIGN, PLEASE!

"I'll put your name in the hat," the promoter promised. "They only give one interview per tour stop, but you'll have as good a chance as anyone else."

"Yeah, right," I thought. "*The Press Register* up against the *Memphis Commercial Appeal* and the *Press Scimitar*, to say nothing of the papers in Little Rock and Tupelo."

Not even taking my autograph book to the show, I found myself sitting third row center. "Not bad," I thought as I settled in. Just as I began to get comfortable, I heard my name on the PA. "Larry Liddell," the voice intoned. "Please, come backstage."

This was the first time I had ever been ASKED to come backstage!

Arriving backstage, I was introduced to Peter, Paul and Mary's road manager who informed me that the group had chosen to grant the interview for the Memphis tour stop to the *Press Register* and that I was to report backstage after the show.

I was excited. And I was scared to death.

Peter, Paul and Mary had been making no bones about their stance on civil rights. They had performed in Washington DC on the day of Martin Luther King's famous "I've Got a Dream" speech, and again in Selma, Alabama, in protest of that state's handling of civil rights. I knew the subject would come up if I got an interview....I just hadn't expected to GET the interview. I went back to my seat and began to prepare myself for the interview.

The concert was one of the best I had ever attended. They performed all the familiar songs and ones that would become familiar for a lifetime. They held nothing back and when it was over, I was once again making my way backstage at the Ellis.

"Here's the routine," the road manager said. "You will talk to them one at a time, in order. They will not be interviewed as a group."

With that, he ushered me into what looked like an interrogation room at a justice center, and I sat down in one of the two chairs placed facing each other. After what seemed like a long time, the door opened and Peter Yarrow walked in, extending his hand. I shook it and he sat down in the other chair, facing me. After about 20 minutes of explaining his philosophies on music, drama and civil rights, he rose as if to leave.

"Could I have your autograph?" I asked timidly.

I then realized I had nothing on which for him to sign. I looked about and saw an old piece of thin cardboard on the floor in the corner of the room. I went over and picked it up, saying sheepishly, "This will have to do."

Smiling, Peter signed: "To Larry, Peter Yarrow."

He left and, momentarily, in walked Paul Stookey.

While Peter was the liberal of the group, Paul was the conservative, and a conservative with a wonderful sense of humor. He kept me laughing throughout the interview and completely put me at ease. We hit it off famously. After signing his name on my cardboard, Paul left and, finally, in walked Mary Travers, the middle-of-the-road member of the group.

"We talk about issues all the time," she told me. "Then we vote on if we want to take a stand and what type of stand do we want to take. We have some heated discussions, too, but in the end, we each vote our conviction and whichever way the vote goes, that's what we do."

As the interview came to an end, I had an inspiration. "Can I ask you for a favor?" I inquired.

"Depends on what it is," she replied suspiciously.

SIGN, PLEASE!

"Can I run my fingers through your hair?"

Mary threw back her head and roared with laughter. "I've been asked for a lot of favors in my time," she said through her laughter," but this is a first! You bet you can! Have at it!"

With that, she just leaned over, her hair falling over her face.

From the first time I had ever see PP&M, I had been mesmerized by Mary's long blonde hair. It looked like corn silk blowin' in the wind (no pun intended), and I always had a hankerin' to run my fingers through it. Doing so was the most fun I ever had with my clothes on! It felt just like it looked. It was pure corn silk. It did not have the feel of hair spray or other chemicals. It was straight, long, over shoulder length, and as beautiful as Mary herself.

By the time Mary signed my cardboard, it was close to midnight. We walked out of the room together to find everybody gone! There was not a soul in the auditorium and upon walking out the stage door, we found that not even one autograph hound had lingered!

Neither Peter, Paul, nor the road manager was in sight.

"Well," Mary sighed wistfully. "It looks like I've been forgotten. Could you give me a ride back to The Peabody?"

I had received a new '64 Oldsmobile Cutlass for graduation, but it certainly wasn't a limousine. And it was neither washed nor all that clean inside, either.

"Sure," I replied, "but my car is in the parking lot down the street, and it's not safe for you to remain here while I go get it. Do you mind walking with me?"

Extending her elbow, she smiled, "I'd be delighted!"

We walked arm-in-arm the one block up to the only car left in the lot. I opened the door for Mary for which she responded, "Such gallantry!"

LARRY LIDDELL

When we arrived at The Peabody, I jumped out and opened Mary's door for her, and then walked with her up the few steps to the hotel door together. Before going into the hotel and out of my life forever, Mary turned and kissed me on the cheek and said, "Thanks, Larry. You were fun." I could have made it back to Clarksdale without the car!

Chapter 14
"Thanks for the Memory"

Two years later, Bob Hope came to Jackson to headline the Mississippi Arts Festival at the new Mississippi Coliseum. The venue was a far cry from the capital city's antiquated old Municipal Auditorium where I'd seen the Limeliters three years earlier.

When I called for press passes, I was told the comedian would hold a press conference immediately before the concert. My credentials would be waiting at "Will Call."

We gathered backstage on an impromptu set, with a couch and a microphone. There were no chairs for the media to sit down, so we stood, anxiously awaiting Hope's arrival. Only a few minutes behind schedule, he appeared, snapplily dressed in a sport coat. And carrying a golf club.

"I'm Bob Hope," he smiled. "You may have heard of me; I'm the guy who carried Bing Crosby in all of those road pictures." Then he asked us all to identify ourselves and tell him where we were from and, "that sort of thing. I like to know who I'm lying to."

Everybody there identified themselves as entertainment writers or editors. When it came my turn, I said, "I'm Larry Liddell, Sports Editor of the Clarksdale Press Register."

His eyes lit up immediately.

"What did you say your title is?" he asked excitedly.

"Sports Editor," I repeated.

"God, it finally happened," he said seriously. "I've been in the business for 30 years, and this is the first time anybody has sent their sports editor to ask me about my golf game!" And with that, he ordered me to join him on the platform.

"You sit right here, Larry," he smiled, helping me onto the couch. Sitting beside me, he said, "Now, what is your first question?

The perfect straight man, I asked, "What is your handicap?"

"Eighteen - holes!" he shot back.

"Did you really play strip poker with Jill St. John in Viet Nam?" I asked. (I had remembered the caption beneath a picture of the actress in his latest book; she was wearing only a towel.)

"I won't talk about my sex life," he quipped with a smile, ""but I'm glad you read my book!"

With that, he looked at me and said, "Now, Larry, I'm going to let these other guys ask me a question or two, but I want you to feel free to jump in at any time with a question about my golf game. OK?" I assured him I would.

Reporters began throwing questions at him about his frequent trips to visit the troops in every war, including and since World War II. Hope was very sincere in his belief that his tours of duty were morale builders for the troops, especially since he always managed to take one or two good-looking

SIGN, PLEASE!

actresses along, a la St. John, Ann Margaret, Connie Stevens, etc.

When one reporter asked him a question critical of the war in Viet Nam, Bob turned to me, hit me in the knee with his golf club, and asked, "Don't you have a question about my golf game? Taking the cue, I asked him to compare his golf swing with that of Arnold Palmer.

"There's really no comparison," he quipped, "as my swing is much more fluid than Arnie's. I'd say about 80 proof fluid." And with that, he stood up, thanked us for coming, and told us to, "enjoy the show." It was then that I offered my autograph book.

"Could you please sign my book?" I asked politely.

"Let me see whose autographs you've got in there," he sat back down.

Looking over the book, he laughed wickedly and said, "I'll sign any book that doesn't have Crosby's signature in it!"

In bold script, he wrote simply, "Bob Hope."

It's bold, but it is *fancy* script!

During the show, Hope asked me to stand up. As the spotlight fell on me, he informed the audience, "Folks, this is the first sports editor ever to attend one of my press conferences. I think he deserves a round of applause for having the good sense to cover a true golfer's press conference!"

The audience howled and gave me a loud ovation, one I'll never forget.

Returning to Clarksdale, I was told that on the following Monday, pianist Peter Nero was appearing in town in the Community Concert series. Next to Liberace, Peter was perhaps our most talented popular music pianist. I was front and center when he was introduced and was simply enthralled by his style and his song list, as was the appreciative local audience in our Municipal Auditorium.

After the concert, I jaunted up and talked with Peter for a while and finished off the chat by handing him my autograph book.

"I was hoping you would ask me to sign it," he smiled, as he took the book and signed, "To Larry, All the Best from Peter Nero."

It was at this juncture of my career that I was leaning toward becoming an entertainment writer, as I was finding these entertainers interesting and intelligent humans. I have never gotten over my desire to meet the stars, although the lure of the sports world won the final battle.

Chapter 15
"Jack, Be Nimble"
PGA MEM

While writing sports for the *Press Register*, I had the opportunity to cover the Memphis Open, then held at the Colonial Country Club. I'd go up every year and come back with some autographs of my favorite golfers. In 1964, for example, I got Arnold Palmer and Gary Player to sign for me. That was special, because if it hadn't been for Arnie, I probably would have ranked golf the same way I do soccer today. Neither was high on my list of sports to cover.

In 1965, I got the third member of the Big Three to sign for me: Jack Nicklaus.

Now, Jack wasn't high on my list, either, as he was beginning to outshine Arnie, the king of golf. Jack was pudgy, from Ohio (meaning he was a Yankee), and, worse, yet, was a graduate of Ohio State. (Arnie might have been from Pennsylvania, but at least he had the good sense to go to Wake Forest, a southern university.)

Jack came out of the pack on that Sunday, May 23, 1965, to tie Johnny Pott, a Mississippi native who was leading, playing two groups behind Jack. Waiting to see if there would be a playoff, Jack came into the press area in the air-conditioned second floor ballroom of the clubhouse.

"Gentlemen," he announced, "I'll answer your questions, but I will be out on the patio. I don't want to cool down in case I have to take part in a playoff."

I was sitting on the patio with other members of the media; while standing in 90-degree heat, Jack was as amiable and nice as Arnie. He fielded every question with ease. I gained a lot of respect for him that day. Sure enough, Pott parred his way home to force a playoff, which Jack won on the second hole.

"Now, I'll answer your questions in the air conditioning," he announced as he entered the press area after the playoff.

Jack sat and answered every question until the last question was asked. He was a gracious as any professional athlete I have ever met. As he was leaving, I walked over and asked him for his autograph.

"Jack Nicklaus," he wrote with a smile.

"Thank you," he said, as he handed the signature back to me.

"No, thank you," I replied with a smile.

Both Arnie and Jack are retired from tournament golf now, and Player is nearing retirement. However, they will always be the Big Three of Golf to me.

Chapter 16
"Cash and the Redhead at Ole Miss"

I left the *Clarksdale Press Register* at the end of 1967 to begin a new career in sports information. The University of Mississippi hired me to be the Assistant Director of Sports Information, to work with Billy Gates who had been the SID at Old Miss ever since he graduated from there in 1938. He was one of the best, and I learned a lot from working with him. The press box at Vaught-Hemingway Stadium is named after Billy who passed away in 1977.

On November 11, 1968, I was notified that I would be in charge of the Tad Smith Coliseum that night, for the Johnny Cash concert. As the newest member of the athletic staff, I was chosen by acclimation. Well, 30 minutes before the 8PM concert, Cash had not arrived, and I was beginning to get nervous. I had a sold-out house with no star. I feared a riot.

Not to worry. A little after 7:30, the Cash tour bus pulled into its appointed spot. The first person off the bus was Cash's wife, June Carter.

"Who's in charge here?" she wanted to know.

"I guess that would be me," I smiled, extending my hand in greeting.

"Do you have any aspirin?" she inquired back, with a smile. "John has a terrible headache. We shouldn't even be here, but he wants to go on."

Nobody wanted him to "go on" more than I did, so I told her I did and showed her where the dressing room was. Then I went in search of aspirin. Finding them in the coach's office, I ran back to the dressing room to find Johnny Cash lying on the couch with a cold rag on his head.

"Thank you, young man," June said, taking the whole bottle of aspirin. "We'll be ready in a few minutes."

The concert began on time, and both John and June were great. They did not cut the show short, singing all their great songs with gusto, kidding around on the stage, much to the delight of both students and the general public.

Security was tight, but several hundred fans gathered around the Cash tour bus after the concert. I went into the dressing room to make sure there was nothing else they needed and to inform them that a crowd was waiting for them.

"We need to get on the road as quickly as possible," June said with that smile. "See what you can do to clear a path for us, please."

Handing her a ticket stub I had snatched from the pile of stubs at one of the gates, I asked for an autograph.

"You have been so nice, sure, we'll sign for you," John said, rising from the couch. "Do you have a pen?" Handing him the stub and my pen, he graciously signed his name and then handed both pen and stub to June, who signed her name as "June Carter Cash."

SIGN, PLEASE!

I went out to alert Security to clear a path and went back inside and walked the pair straight to the door of the bus. Neither stopped to sign an autograph. I quickly scurried back inside the coliseum and began the long wait for the clean-up crew to finish its job before locking up. My only activity was to look at the treasured signatures I had secured.

My time on the Ole Miss staff coincided with the sophomore, junior and senior seasons for Archie Manning, one of the most heralded quarterbacks in school history. Archie got a lot of ink while at Ole Miss and brought a lot of sports writers to Oxford during those three years. And he brought a guy who was not your average sports writer.

Heywood Hale Broun, a mustachioed fellow, was a special correspondent for CBS, and Archie's junior season was phenomenal, setting the stage for a possible bid for the Heisman Trophy. Broun called Gates and arranged to interview the redhead, but when the CBS crew arrived, I was appointed to take charge and handle Broun while he was in town. He had a reputation for being difficult to work with, demanding this and that in a dictatorial manner. His public relations people must have put out that word, because I found him to be an intellectual, entertaining and very knowledgeable about sports and other topics.

Once he finished interviewing Arch, I took Broun back to the Oxford Inn with every intention of dropping him off with a final Hotty Toddy, and that would be it. Broun invited me to have dinner with him and after dinner invited me to his room to watch the interview on TV. As we settled down in his room, he brought a bottle of Jack Daniels out of his suitcase, secured cokes and 7-ups, and we shared the bottle of Jack while viewing the afternoon interview.

LARRY LIDDELL

I got home around midnight that night, a lot better informed about several subjects than I was before the evening began. Broun was one of the smartest members of the national media to visit Oxford. And before leaving, he signed one of his personal cards for me.

Chapter 17
"That Girl"

The Shower of Stars, a Danny Thomas spectacular connected with the Memphis Open, was a gold mine for an autograph hound like me. Dinah Shore had been gracious enough to give me an autograph in 1970 after the show. One day when I was sitting at my desk minding my own business, Early Maxwell, a Memphis promoter who handled a lot of the program ads for Ole Miss Athletics, called me.

"Are you coming up for the Shower of Stars?" he asked, knowing full well that I was, since he'd already promised me a ticket. The event was held in conjunction with the Danny Thomas/St. Jude Open Golf Tournament. Assuring him that I was, he asked me if I wanted a date.

"Who with?" was my reply

"I can't tell you that," he said weakly.

"I don't like blind dates, Early," I assured him, "especially when I don't even know her name."

"Trust me, you'll like her," he said mischievously. "It's just that her father swore me to secrecy, and I am desperate. I have got to find this girl a date, and I've been turned down more often than a bed sheet at the Peabody."

"I'll bet you have," I laughed at his situation.

"Please, Larry, you've got to trust me on this one, he begged. "I'll guarantee you won't regret it." Early had been nice to me many times over the years, so I relented and said yes.

"Do you have a tux?" he asked suddenly.

"A tux? Come on, Early, you didn't say anything about a tux," I literally screamed.

"Get a tux and plan to be at the Holiday Inn RiverMont at 3PM the Saturday of the show," he continued giving me orders. "You'll take a limo to the airport and meet her at 4PM at the charter terminal."

"Meet who?" I shot back, a little upset that not only would I have to wear a zoot suit, but I would also miss an afternoon of the golf tournament.

"That girl," Early said with a smile in his voice.

"What girl?" I shot back, exasperated.

"*That* girl," he said calmly. It was then that I caught on.

Danny Thomas' daughter, Marlo, was starring in a TV sitcom called, "That Girl." Early had set me up with Marlo.

"Are you talking about…" I began.

"Shhhhh," he cut me off. "Don't say a word. Remember, this is top secret."

He then shared my itinerary with me. On schedule, I arrived at the RiverMont, the flagship of the Holiday Inn chain, at 3PM. Just before 4, I saw this long white limo out front and went out and asked if it was waiting for me. The driver said that, indeed, he was waiting for me.

SIGN, PLEASE!

We went straight to the airport charter terminal, and a private jet was just taxiing in as we drove onto the tarmac. Hopping out of the limo, I literally ran toward the plane as the door opened, and she popped out.

"Hi," I said as she got to the bottom of the steps.

"Hi, Larry," she smiled, those big black eyes beaming. I was on notice that she had been briefed about me, too. She was just as bubbly in person as she was on TV, talking and laughing all the way back to the hotel.

"I'll be ready at 6," she said with a smile.

"That's a little early," I objected. The show wasn't until 7:30, and Early had arranged for dinner at 9:30 at Justine's, a now-defunct but then five-star restaurant.

Without a blink of an eye, she replied, "We are having cocktails with Daddy at 6 in the Penthouse."

"Oh," was all I could muster. (How many other details has Early left out of this arrangement, I wondered.)

As promised, she was ready at six, and we went up to the Penthouse. A waiter opened the door, and Marlo ran into the room, gushing, ":Daddy, it's so good to see you?"

"You must be Larry," he spoke curtly as he shook my hand. Releasing his hand, I found a $100 bill in my palm.

"I don't need this, sir," and handed it back to him.

"I like this boy already," he laughed, pocketing the C-note. Finally, it was time to leave for the Coliseum. We left the hotel and got into the limo for the ride out.

"Thank you," Marlo grabbed my hand,

"For what?" I answered. After all, I hadn't done anything.

"For not taking that money," she smiled. "He just wants the guys who escort me on the road to be able to show me a good time. It makes for some awkward moments."

75

"Don't worry," I smiled, "I promise we'll have a good time!"

Standing backstage at the Coliseum, I felt a tap on my shoulder. Looking around, I found myself staring into the blue eyes of Frank Sinatra.

"Are you with her?" he asked seriously, pointing to Marlo. Gulping, I replied, "Yessir."

"You touch her, and I'll kill you," he scowled.

Turning around, Marlo laughed, "Oh, Uncle Frank, you are such a comic." Whew, I thought. He sure had me fooled! The show was wonderful, as was the meal at Justine's.

On the way back to the hotel, Marlo asked, "Do you dance?" The truth was, "Not much."

"Oh, I'll bet you know all the hot spots in Memphis,": she laughed. "Tell you what, let's dump the limo, grab your car, and go dancing." After a quick two-hour spin of the top dancing spots in Memphis, we returned to the hotel at 3AM. Thinking this was it, I said goodnight after opening the door to her suite.

"See you at 9," she smiled.

"Uh?" I was caught unaware again.

"You are going to take me to the golf tournament tomorrow, aren't you?" she smiled.

"Oh, sure," I said, "see you at 9."

The next day went by in a whirl. Provided with a golf cart, we whizzed all over Colonial Country Club, seeing as many of the golfers as we could while trying to avoid the crowd. She shared her time with Danny who also had a cart.

After presenting Dave Hill with the winner's check, Marlo hopped back into our golf cart and said, "To the airport, James!"

SIGN, PLEASE!

"I don't remember telling you my first name is James," I looked at her quizzically.

"Is it really?" she threw back her head and laughed. "I must be psychic!" Psychic? No.

A dream to be around? Absolutely. The limo pulled up to the plane, and while Marlo's luggage was being stowed in the plane, we sat in the limo telling each other what a wonderful week-end it had been. I was telling the truth. If she was lying, I couldn't tell.

With a good-bye kiss, Marlo bounded up the steps to the plane and, turning, blew another kiss my way before disappearing into the aircraft. Her energy level had never dipped below 100% since she had arrived the day before.

The next day, Early called me.

"Was I right?" I could tell he was busting a gut to keep from laughing.

"Damned right," I exclaimed. "That was the only blind date I ever enjoyed and one I'll never forget. Thanks, Early."

"Thank you," he shot back quickly. "You were my last hope. I would have died of embarrassment if I hadn't gotten her an escort!"

"Just don't tell those other guys who they turned down," I laughed.

"Don't worry," he replied. "They'll never know."

Chapter 18
"The Saints Came Marchin' In"

In February of 1971, Archie's friends and followers gave him his "day" in his hometown of Drew, Mississippi, a tiny Delta hamlet about 15 miles east of Cleveland. As the Ole Miss press coordinator for the day, I was there to handle the many photo opportunities and interviews for the horde of media reps attending the event.

Also there was J. D. Roberts, head coach of the New Orleans Saints, the team that had drafted Arch in the NFL earlier that month. With Roberts was the team's player personnel director, Henry Lee Parker, brother-in-law of Dave "Boo" Ferris. Henry Lee introduced me to Roberts, and I took him over and introduced him to members of the media. I lined up Arch to pose for a picture or two with his new coach. While the media was busy with the pair, Henry Lee casually asked me if I would be interested in interviewing for the assistant PR director's position with the Saints, and I said sure, why not.

SIGN, PLEASE!

Two weeks later, I was invited to New Orleans to talk with the team's general manager, Vic Schwenk, and Harry Hulmes, the team PR director. At the Memphis Airport the morning of the interview, I learned that my Aunt Onie had passed away in Shreveport. The Saints showed their class when they rearranged my itinerary. I returned to Memphis via Shreveport to attend her funeral.

Two weeks after that, I got a call from Larry McMillen, a sports writer for the New Orleans *Times Picayune* newspaper. It was 11PM, and I was already asleep. After identifying himself, Larry asked, "What do you have to say about being the Saints' Assistant Public Relations Director?"

Stunned, I said, "I can't say anything, because I haven't been offered the position."

"Well, you will be tomorrow, and I'm on deadline, so say something, or I'll quote you as saying, 'no comment.'" he laughed.

"I'm honored to be considered for the position," I laughed.

The next morning, after reading the *Times,* Hulmes called me, apologized for the "leak," and offered me the position. I accepted and moved to New Orleans and began at my new post April 1, 1971.

Al Hirt was a minority owner of the NFL team and owned a club on Bourbon Street in the French Quarter. Saints personnel were always welcome in his club. One night, I was approached by a really big guy who introduced himself by saying, "I hear you are a member of the New Orleans Saints."

Assuring him that I was only the team's PR guy, he challenged me to arm wrestle him. Our team photographer, Erby Aucoin, was with me and stepped in to try and diffuse the situation.

After some tense negotiation, the guy smiled, extended his hand and said, "I'm Leif Erickson, and I'm filming a movie in your town, and I'm out for a little R&R between takes."

I have long since forgotten the name of the movie, but I still have the autograph on the back of one of my business cards. It reads, "To Liddell with love, Leif Erickson."

When I questioned the 'with love' notation, he roared with laughter. "Just to show you I am a peace-loving man." Erickson's co-star was with him that night, and Erby got his autograph for me on the back of one of his cards, but for the life of me, to this day I can't make it out!

Also with Leif that night was an actor who appeared in many John Wayne movies and other westerns, including one called, "The Wild Bunch." His name was Ben Johnson, and he was having fun that night, too. He took one of my cards but kept it. A couple of weeks later, I received an envelope from Hollywood. Opening it, I was thrilled to discover a personally autographed picture of Johnson, in my opinion, one of the best character actors ever to appear on the silver screen.

Up the street from Hirt's club in the Quarter was clarinetist Pete Fountain's club. Pete was a favorite of mine from his days with Lawrence Welk. In fact, it if hadn't been for Pete, I probably never would have seen Welk's show, until, that is, the Lennon Sisters joined the show. Anyway, one day I received a phone call from Pete's agent saying that Pete would like me to join him for a cruise on the Mississippi River. I had seen Pete perform once at Mississippi State College for Women and once in his Bourbon Street digs, but I'd never met him. That was one of the perks of being with the Saints. You got all these neat invites from out of the blue.

So, bearing my autograph book, I boarded his big boat (he insisted on the term boat rather than yacht) and we set sail.

SIGN, PLEASE!

Pete was so interesting to talk to, I hardly even noticed the river at all. We must have talked for four hours, and just before we docked, I extended my book and asked for his autograph. Even after several shots of our favorite hootch, he signed a perfect, "All the Best, Pete Fountain."

One Sunday afternoon in old Tulane Stadium, team owner John Mecom entertained actor Paul Newman in his private box. As the game was winding down, the actor strolled down into the press box and asked me for a "book" on the game. The "book" was a play-by-play of the game, complete with statistics, quotes, etc.

I looked into his steely blue eyes and said, "I'll give you one, if you will autograph one for me."

"I don't think so," he smiled, "but I'll mail you one when I get back home."

I thought nothing of this exchange until an envelope arrived for me about two weeks later. Sure enough, it was a personally autographed picture of the academy award-winning actor. Unfortunately, it was in black and white and didn't highlight Paul's baby blues.

A couple of years later, I was in the press box at the Coliseum in Los Angeles when I spotted Ross Martin, co-star with Robert Conrad of the TV hit, "Wild, Wild West." Ross was just enjoying the ball game from the press box. I strolled up and casually asked him for his autograph on a piece of paper I pulled out of a reporter's notebook. "All the Best, Ross Martin" he wrote with a smile.

"Thank you," he said, handing it back to me.

"No, thank you," I smiled.

We then engaged in a conversation that, looking back on it, could have changed my life forever. He told me how he came to be an actor, and I told him I had some acting experience (the lead in my high school senior play and two community theater productions). He asked if I was interested in an acting career.

"Oh, if the money's right," I laughed, never thinking he was serious.

"Well, we are looking for a guy about your size and with your accent to play a recurring role on 'West,' and I believe I could get you a shot at it if you are interested," he said seriously. "You get killed after three episodes, but it would be a shot at the business. How about it?"

I couldn't speak for what was going through my mind. Here it is, I thought, my shot at stardom. I could see myself getting an Emmy for the role (that was a given) and going on to bigger and better things. At the same time, the thought crossed my mind that (1) I had the best job I had ever had by that point in my life, (2) I had a wife and child to support and (3) a house note and car note, etc. I must be out of my mind to even think about leaving all that to take a chance on an acting career.

"I'll have to pass, but thanks a million for even considering me for the part," I said humbly.

"You'll probably regret that decision one day, but I know what you're thinking, and at the moment, it sounds like the right decision," he smiled, extending his hand. I took his hand in gratitude and thought about that meeting every time I watched an episode of "Wild, Wild West."

I never did see an episode featuring someone with a southern accent in a recurring role who was killed off after three episodes.

Chapter 19
"I Go To Hollywood"

Hollywood was a favorite NFL stop for me, if not for the Saints. They had very little success against the Rams when I was with the franchise. Once, the Rams shut us out 35-0, and upon returning to New Orleans, we were greeted by a raucous crowd of Charlie's Marching Saints, who were always at the airport to greet us, win or lose. However, on this particular night, there were a lot more uniformed New Orleans policemen than usual among those waiting for us at the end of the concourse.

"I wonder what all the policemen are here for," I wondered aloud.

John North, the team's head coach, didn't miss a beat. "Probably here to arrest us for impersonating a professional football team," he shot back.

For an autograph collector, the LA area was heaven. One time, I was driving down a street in my rental car and had to stop for a red light. Looking to the car on my left, there was actress Doris Day, smiling back at me from the wheel of her convertible.

Once, a group of us were at a fashionable Hollywood eatery when I noticed James Caan getting out of a limo in front of the restaurant. I grabbed my business cards and made for the front door, bumping into a guy who was entering. I ran up to Caan and asked him for his signature and saying, "Sure," with a smile, signed "James Caan" on the back of my card. This was the year after he should have won an Oscar for his portrayal of Sonny Corleone in "The Godfather."

When I returned to my table, Eddie Jones, the team's business manager, asked me if I knew who I had almost knocked down getting to Caan.

"No, who?" I inquired.

"Don Adams," he laughed with the rest of the table. Adams was then star of a hit TV show called, "Get Smart." Undaunted, I walked over to Adams' table, apologized, and got his autograph, too!

The Saints stayed at the Sheraton Universal when playing the Rams, and the hotel was a virtual off-lot-studio for Universal Studios. I saw many stars shoot scenes around the pool, in the lobby, etc. I got to see James Garner shoot a scene from his mega hit, "The Rockford Files." The hotel lobby had been turned into an airport gate area, and Rockford was walking from the waiting area to a ticket counter. He walked past the hotel gift shop which, of course, resembled the gift shop at the airport. He spread his arms like a plane and sidestepped into the gift shop.

"Cut," the director screamed. "Jim, what are you doing?"

"You know I can't pass up a gift shop at an airport," he smiled at the frustrated director.

SIGN, PLEASE!

On another occasion, I was in the hotel restaurant having lunch while a TV crew was visible through the restaurant window, shooting around the pool. It didn't take long to spot George Peppard and realize it was a scene being shot for his hot TV detective show, "Banacek." The scene was shot, and the crew broke for lunch. Peppard came into the restaurant looking for a table, which was impossible. The place was packed. I raised my arm high into the air, getting his attention. He came over.

"Feel free to join me if you'd like," I said, handing him one of my business cards.

"Thank you very much," he said as he sat down.

We enjoyed a delightful lunch, after which he signed his name on a small piece of paper he attained from somewhere. I insisted on paying for lunch, making him a Saints' fan for life, I'm sure.

One day, I returned to the hotel from my daily rounds of working the media to find baseball hall of famer Dizzy Dean sitting in the lobby.

"Diz," I extended my hand and introduced myself, "what are you doing out here?"

"Partner, I'm about to blow a gasket," he shot back with a scowl. "I'm out here to be on the Carson show tonight, and the network was supposed to get me a room here, but there are no rooms available, so I guess I'm going to spend the night in the lobby."

"Let me see what I can do," I said.

"I'd very much appreciate anything you can do, partner," he smiled. "I'm as tired as a possum that's been chased by a coon dog!"

Ross Bell was the resident manager of the hotel and a good friend of mine. I went to the desk and got him on the phone.

Momentarily, a bellman walked up to where Diz and I were chatting, offering a room key.

"Welcome to the Sheraton Universal," the bellman said.

"Man, you got clout," Dizzy laughed, shaking my hand.

"Courtesy of the New Orleans Saints," I said proudly. "We Southern boys have to stick together."

"You're right about that, partner," he said with a smile, as he followed the bellman to the elevators.

The room was secured courtesy of the Saints, but paid for by NBC, I assure you.

Chapter 20
"Hollywood Comes to New Orleans"

There were two Super Bowls held in New Orleans during my tenure with the Saints, and both games brought many celebrities to the Crescent City. Some we who had relatives in the city came to visit during Super Bowl week. Phil Harris, the actor-comedian, was one of those. His daughter and her husband lived on the west bank, and Phil flew in for both Super Bowls. I ran into Phil at one of the many fine restaurants in the French Quarter one evening as I was making my rounds of watering holes. Phil was visiting an old friend of his, Fred McMurray, in McMurray's suite at the Royal Orleans.

Offering him one of my business cards, I asked Phil for his autograph. Without a word, he took the card, flipped it over to make sure it was a legitimate card, and signed, "Good Wishes, Phil Harris." I like to think he meant it.

"Are you a collector?" he asked suddenly.

"Yes, I am," I replied.

"Well, go in the lobby bar and you'll find my good friend, Fred McMurray, sitting next to the window," he confided with a smile. "Be sure and get his."

Thanking him profusely, I hustled into the bar and, sure enough, there was the unmistakable profile of McMurray, whom I recognized for his TV role on, "My Three Sons," and for his fine performance in, "Double Indemnity" on the big screen.

Casually walking up to him as he sipped his drink, I asked, "Mr. McMurray, may I have your autograph?"

"Sit down and join me, please," he said with a smile.

We engaged in conversation just long enough for me to buy us a drink and chatted about football, although I did manage to ask him a few questions about his movie work, like who was the best-looking actress he had ever worked with.

"Carol Lombard," he said without hesitation. "Maybe not the best actress, though she wasn't bad, but, without doubt, the best looking of 'em all."

He also had high praise for his "Indemnity" co-star, Barbara Stanwyck. "She was well thought of as an actress," he said, adding, "but she was a very underrated actress, in my opinion."

McMurray's opinion was born out later by the fact that Miss Stanwyck was given the Honorary Lifetime Achievement Award in 1982, although she never won an Oscar.

Mr Murray's autograph reminds me of Hollywood politics every time I look at it.

Jim Nabors was a very good friend of Saints' owner John Mecom, and the two visited each other frequently. One day I was sitting at my desk going over the latest team statistics when I was interrupted by someone knocking on my desk. I had been so intent on the stats that I didn't hear anybody come

SIGN, PLEASE!

into my office. Looking up, I found myself staring at the face of —- Gomer Pyle!

"Hi," he said with a smile. "I was wondering if you could tell me how to get to John's apartment."

Mecom had an apartment on the third floor of the Saints' Lee Circle office building where he could stay when not in his Houston River Oaks home, or on his ranch in Mexico, The apartment was accessible by a private elevator located in an alcove near the front of the building.

"I can show you," I said eagerly.

"I'm Jim Nabors," he announced unnecessarily but humbly, extending his hand.

Giving him my card, I told him who I was and what my job was with the organization. He seemed sincerely interested as we strolled down the hall. I rode up to the apartment with him and was invited to stay for a drink. We seemed to click, and I enjoyed the moment.

Later, at Mardi Gras in 1974, my wife and I were guests of John and his wife Katsy in their apartment above the parade route. We caught stuff from floats and threw miniature Saints footballs to the crowd below. It was one of the best Mardi Gras we ever experienced. At some point during the day, Jim Nabors joined the party, and he, too, got into the spirit of the occasion and had a great time. As luck would have it, we left the apartment at the same time as Jim. My wife, Martha, blinked those baby blue eyes of hers at him and said, "I just love your theme song, 'Tomorrow Never Comes.'" Within seconds, as the elevator door closed, Jim got down on one knee and sang the first verse and chorus of the song a cappella, without missing a note! It was one of the most poignant moments of our lives, one that neither of us will ever forget. And it meant more than an autograph ever would.

Chapter 21
"Hello, Dolly"

The Blue Room at the Fairmont Hotel provided me with many chances to mingle with celebrities over the years in New Orleans. I remember very well one night taking Martha and our daughter Stephanie to see Carol Channing, the wonderful Broadway actress. I had seen her in my first time to see a Broadway play, "Hello, Dolly," in 1964.

Carol was making the showroom circuit now with a Las Vegas-type show in which she sang, danced, told stories — both funny and sad — and just entertained for about 90 minutes. After the show, she made her way toward our table and shook our hands and invited us up to her suite!

Unbeknownst to us, Marilyn Barnett, the top-notch public relations director for the hotel, had told Carol that I was her counterpart with the Saints and a big fan. We accepted Carol's invitation to come up to her suite and chat after the show. She was so gracious, rightfully paying more attention to Martha than me, bestowing diamonds on our daughter by the handful!

SIGN, PLEASE!

It was quite a night, but another time when asking for an autograph seemed inappropriate.

Yet another Blue Room memory was provided by dancer/actor Ben Vereen, an African-American performer who was among the first of his ilk to play the hotel showroom in the civil-rights era. Although I have no knowledge that she did, I believe that Marilyn had told Ben that I was going to be in attendance that evening, and where I'd be sitting, as he seemed to play to our table all night.

Martha and I had brought her parents, Frank and Hazel Howell, with us on this particular night. Hazel adored Vereen as much as Martha and Frank and I did. We all admired his fancy footwork and acting ability as well. That night, Ben outdid himself. His performance was great, and he received a standing ovation. As we were preparing to leave, Ben came off the stage, thanked us for coming, and leaned over and kissed my wife!!

Emmitt Till was murdered for just whistling at a white woman in 1955 at a grocery store in Money, Mississippi, about 40 miles from Cleveland where I was living then. Here it was, 20 years later, and a black man felt free enough in New Orleans to kiss a married white woman in front of 500 folks! Then Ben smiled and reached out his hand to me, which I immediately shook with an even bigger smile. This was a fine testimony as to how far the South had come in race relations.

Chapter 22
"I'm in Love with Reba McEntire" (and my wife knows it!)

The red-headed country singer grabbed me by the ears in the early 80's and has never let go. I believe the first song I heard her sing was, "You're the First Time I Thought about Cheating," a typical country song. It was delivered in such a powerful way by this Oklahoma-born rodeo girl that it was impossible not to listen and admire the whole song.

I first saw Reba in '86 at the University of New Orleans. I'd been listening to her on FJM 101.1 WNOE radio for four years and was very excited to be seeing her in person. Brooks and Dunn opened the show. It was the first time I'd ever heard of them, much less seen them, and they impressed me, too. I told the lady sitting by me, "These guys are going to go places!" Little did I know just how far Brooks and Dunn would go! And Miss Reba put on quite a show that night, changing costumes something like 14 times during her 70-minute performance.

SIGN, PLEASE!

I next saw Reba in Baton Rouge, and oh…what a night THAT was!

I had talked my wife, Martha, into accompanying me to the Baton Rouge show, after I'd been bending her ear about Reba for 5 years while trying to persuade her to come along to a live show. I gobbled up two tickets to Reba's Red Stick Show, and away we went.

Well, wouldn't you know it? That evening, it snowed!! One of the rare snowfalls ever in Baton Rouge, only 70 miles west of sultry New Orleans, and Martha was in no mood for snow.

She'd just built up enough interest in seeing Reba live, and now I was asking her to endure a snowstorm!

Blessed woman that she is, Martha came along, only after I promised her we wouldn't return to Kenner in the snow. I booked us a room at The Marriott Courtyard in Baton Rouge. We checked in and then left for the Centroplex. We stood freezing in line in the snow for half an hour before the merciless staff finally opened the outer doors, and Martha was fit to be tied.

The concert was great, of course, but Martha was neither amused nor entertained. She thawed out just in time to trek back out in the snow to the car for the ride back to The Courtyard. I have never lived that night down.

In '94, when I was working in Lafayette LA, I got word that Reba was going to be in Lake Charles, a mere 60 miles away. I immediately drove over to purchase a ticket. I told the ticket seller at the convention center, "As close to the stage as I can get." Because I had a plan.

My seat was on Row 5, just to the right of the stage in the Loge Section. I wore my red jacket, made famous during my days with the Louisiana Association of Fairs and Festivals.

And since I was the only fan wearing a red jacket, I sort of stood out in the crowd, which was my plan.

As Reba sang "The Telephone Song," she turned and pointed straight at me as she belted out the line, "Why haven't I heard from you?" It was a thrill to me to have 12,000 people look at me and wonder, "Does she really know that guy?" Of course, she didn't...but THEY didn't know that!

In '95, I got an even bigger thrill, thanks to a tip I had gotten at the Lake Charles show. I had noticed that some folks were wearing REBA MEET & GREET labels, so I asked what that meant. They said they were members of Reba's fan club and had been selected to meet her after the show. Well, the very next day, I joined her fan club....and then I waited.

When they posted the dates for her '95 tour, New Orleans was on the schedule, so I applied for a ticket to the MEET & GREET. Two days before the concert, I was notified that I'd been selected as one to go backstage and meet Reba.

Imagine my excitement when she entered the room and began addressing each one of us as she strolled down the center aisle. When it came my turn, I just smiled and thanked her for coming to New Orleans, and she replied with a bright smile, "Why, thank you. It's one of my favorite cities to visit!" I realize she says that about every city, but she sure sounded as if she meant it, and I sure did!

Reba made it clear that night that it's unfortunate that she does not sign autographs due to time constraints. This was a disappointment, to say the least.

In '99, I was moving from New Orleans to Clarksdale and was, at the time, President-elect of the Louisiana Lung Association. I had served that organization for many years, as a volunteer, then on the Board and as Vice-President. Reba was the American Lung Association spokesperson for '99.

SIGN, PLEASE!

At my final Board meeting, the Association presented me with a sheet of Christmas Seals, personally autographed by Reba!

Now, knowing I have her autograph, I breathe much easier!

Chapter 23
"Lonely are the Brave"

Children's Hospital in New Orleans is a fun place to work. There's the annual Miracle Network Telethon benefiting Children's Hospitals nationwide. There is Mardi Gras which brings famous and infamous people to town each year. And, once-upon-a-time, there was Celebration Uptown, a two-day festival that featured many of the local musicians that *are* New Orleans. As director of Celebration Uptown, it was my job to round up talent for the event.

The star of the week-end was always the great diva, the Soul Queen of New Orleans, Miss Irma Thomas. She closed the festival every year on Sunday night, drawing large crowds that put us over the top in our fund-raising efforts. Celebration Uptown, thanks in large part to Irma, netted over $60,000 each year for the hospital.

I never asked for an autograph from any of the stars I booked; however, it was a pleasure for me to shake the hands of The Neville Brothers, Dr. John, The Blues Brothers, Frankie Brent, and Frankie Ford, along with Irma.

Of course, as soon as I left Children's Hospital, I dropped off the radar scope of most of these celebs, but not Irma's. Irma still speaks to me when we run across each other these days, and as far as I'm concerned, that's not often enough.

Once, when Irma was appearing at Casino Magic in Bay St. Louis, Mississippi, I got in line to buy one of her CD's. Asking for her to autograph it, she recognized my voice and looking up, smiled, "Don't you ever stand in line to get my autograph again, Larry. You just ask."

Also, the King of Bacchus visits Children's Hospital each year on the Sunday prior to Fat Tuesday. I had the pleasure of escorting two of the kings on tours of the hospital when they visited — Charlton Heston and Kirk Douglas. Heston was in a hurry to get into his costume and wasn't much of a talker. He seemed to enjoy visiting with the sick children and never cut short a stop in a patient's room

Douglas, on the other hand, was in a talkative mood and zipped around the hospital like he had been there before. I asked him what his favorite movie role had been, knowing that my favorite Kirk Douglas movie was, "Lonely are the Brave."

Imagine my shock when he said, "A little known flick about a horse called, 'Lonely are the Brave.' I just love that movie to this day," he retorted with a melancholy smile.

"Mine, too," I muttered, disappointed that I couldn't have said it first.

"Really?" he smiled. "I'm pleased that you saw it. It is sort of an obscure film, but I fell in love with that horse during the filming and bought it when the shoot was over."

And I thought Roy Rogers was the only star who had done that!

Chapter 24
"The Stars Shine for Charity"

Before working at Children's Hospital, I was for two years the Director of Public Relations for the Easter Seal Society of Louisiana. This provided me an opportunity to make my first trip to Las Vegas, a town to which I became instantly attached. I vowed to return and have done so several times. This was another venue in which it did not seem ethical to ask celebs for autographs, as they were appearing gratis to help handicapped children and adults. Still, the job threw me with celebrities of all kinds.

One of the most bizarre was Wolfman Jack whose real name was Robert Smith.

This famous Hollywood disc jockey was the national spokesperson for Easter Seals in 1980. One of the special events I created especially for Wolfman was a Dance-a-Thon, a 24-hour marathon dance program for teenagers.

Staged in cooperation with Hammond Square Mall, we held the Dance-a-Thon in Hammond, Louisiana, about 30 miles

SIGN, PLEASE!

outside of New Orleans. To get to Hammond, it was necessary to cross the swamps that skirt Lake Pontchatrain. The event was held in late February/early March before Daylight Savings Time kicked in. Wolfman's plane didn't arrive in NOLA until 8PM, the scheduled start time for the event.

I was at the Mall, getting the contestants registered, and had an associate waiting at the airport to escort Wolfman to Hammond in a limo. Wolfman arrived at the Mall just before 10PM, looking a little haggard and agitated.

"Man," he said, as he gripped my hand, "I thought I was being kidnapped! No one told me this gig was in a swamp!"

Much to the delight of the contestants, Wolfman Jack took over the microphone and actually spent the entire night spinning records and telling stories as the teens danced the night away to the tunes of the era, such as "I Love the Night Life," by Donna Summers and "September Morn," by Neil Diamond, among many other favorites.

Another star I met through my association with Easter Seals was the great composer/pianist Marvin Hamlisch who graciously gave his autograph. Marvin came to a gig benefiting Easter Seals at a music store in downtown New Orleans.

Hamlisch was a perfectionist and couldn't find a piano that was in key at the store. We had to phone out for a piano tuner to come to the store and tune a piano for Marvin to play. Once the tuning was done, however, the music that came forth from that piano was incredible, let me tell you. All of the television stations in the city were there and featured him on the 6 and 10 o'clock news shows that evening and, just like that, another special event and another special star had helped raise money for the Easter Seal Society.

I shudder to think what would have happened if that piano tuner had been out of pocket!

LARRY LIDDELL

I must give a pat on the back to another talented pianist before I leave my Easter Seals era. Pianist Ronnie Kole served on the board for the Louisiana East Seal Society, and I really don't know what we would have done without him. Ronnie worked like a Trojan helping to build the organization into the giant that it is today in Louisiana: he not only performed regularly and on the annual Easter Seal telethon. Ronnie recruited other musicians to do the same. Yet another hero I never asked for an autograph

Chapter 25
"The Statler Brothers at Miss. State"

Between the Saints and Easter Seals, I sold insurance for a year back in Oxford, Mississippi. I managed to acquire tickets to a Statler Brothers concert in Starkville, home of Ole Miss' arch-rival, the Mississippi State Bulldogs. Martha and our daughter Stephanie went with me that memorable night. The concert was great, as were all Statler Brothers shows.

After the concert, the Brothers announced that they would come back and "sign stuff for as long as there was stuff to sign" right in front of the stage. Stephanie wanted to go down and get their autographs, so I said, "Sure, go ahead." Moments later, she returned, in tears. One of the MSU security guards had blocked her from getting to the floor, telling her that "only those seated on the floor were allowed to get autographs."

Incensed, I picked Stephanie up and carried her back to the railing and lifted her over the barrier onto the floor, while the security guard glared. As she ran toward the stage, I glared back at the security guard, saying, "I hope you arrest me. I'll own this place."

Back home the next day, I wrote a letter to The Statler Brothers at their headquarters in Staunton, Virginia, never thinking I'd get a reply. About 10 days later, I got an envelope with a letter of apology and autographed pictures of each of the Statlers. Shortly after this, we moved back to New Orleans where I joined the staff of the Easter Seal Society of Louisiana.

A year later, I came home one day to find an envelope in my mailbox addressed to me with a return address of Mississippi State University, Starkville, Mississippi. I remarked to my wife that somebody at MSU had learned to type! Opening it, I was stunned to find four tickets to that year's Statler Brothers show at MSU, with a letter apologizing for "last year's incident" and hoping I would return for another Statler Brothers show. Unfortunately, by the time I got the letter, it was too late for us to get to the show. However, I will always remember it as a class act on the part of not only the Statler Brothers but also Mississippi State University.

A year after that, the Statler Brothers appeared in Shreveport on the same night as the annual Easter Seal Telethon. I made my way out to the Fairgrounds and got backstage to the group's dressing area, where I was welcomed as I asked for 25 autographed pictures to auction off at the telethon that night.

"Heck, yeah, we'll do that," Harold Reid said gleefully. "Get Barbara in here. She needs to get in on this opportunity." Barbara Mandrell was the group's opening act that night, and she came right in and signed 25 of her pictures, too.

While they were signing, we made small talk, and I mentioned the Mississippi State fiasco. "I remember reading your letter," Don Reid, the lead singer and Harold's brother recalled. "Did you get the tickets Mississippi State sent you?"

SIGN, PLEASE!

I told them I had and although I couldn't go, I appreciated the gesture."

"It was more than a gesture," Don said flatly. "I'm glad you were here tonight. We looked for you at MSU this year and were afraid you never got the tickets."

I was overwhelmed. They were sincere about correcting the error that had been made long after sending me their apology and autographs a year earlier!

How often does one experience that level of sincerity in show business?

Chapter 26
"Truly a True Value"

The Country Showdown is a talent contest held yearly nationwide to find top country music talent. I was fortunate enough to be asked to judge the Louisiana finals of this contest when it was sponsored by True Value Hardware.

As luck would have it, country singer Laurie Morgan was the national spokesperson for True Value and the Showdown, and True Value just happened to stage their annual convention that year in New Orleans. Backstage, before her concert at the convention, I was the last person in line to get an autographed picture of Laurie.

While she was signing, I mentioned that I was sorry about the death of Laurie's, husband, Keith Whitley. Tearing up, she acknowledged my comment and went into an elaborately detailed story about what had happened, telling me some of the measures she had taken to try and curtail Keith's drinking problem.

SIGN, PLEASE!

"I even tied the belt of my robe around his ankle and the other end around mine so I would know if he got up during the night," she said. "I told him he needed professional help, and he said he'd kill me if I had him committed. I did everything I could."

"I'm sure you did, Laurie," I managed with a smile. "God bless you and good luck."

Walking away, my wife gave me hail Columbia.

"Why did you have to say anything about her husband's death?" she asked.

"I was just trying to acknowledge the fact that I felt bad about the death of her husband," I confessed. "I didn't realize it would trigger a flashback."

J. H. Martin, who runs the Greater Baton Rouge State Fair, and his wife Pat were with us, and he suggested what I believe to be the situation: "I think she was moved that someone outside of show business would comment on Keith being her husband and not just a fine country singer,"

Chapter 27
"Tiny Bubbles"

One of the more recent autographs I collected belongs to a gentleman who passed away in 2007 — Don Ho.

I was attending the National Association of Counties annual meeting in Honolulu, Hawaii, and as I usually do when on the road, I was thumbing through the phone book to see if I recognized any names from my past. You never know who's living where these days. It was a Sunday night, and my wife had not accompanied me to paradise. She does not like to fly, especially when the flight is eight hours long!

Anyway, as I thumbed through the H's, I came across the name Ho, Don and saw a number.

"I wonder if that's the same Don Ho who sang 'Tiny Bubbles' all those years ago," I thought.

The next listing in the book told me that it, indeed, was the same guy. "Ho, Don Theater" the listing read. The next day, I dialed the theater.

"Is Don singing tonight?" I asked?

SIGN, PLEASE!

"No," was the reply. "He doesn't appear on Monday nights."

"How about tomorrow night?" I asked

"Sure," the voice said. "How many in your party?"

"Just me, and I can sit at the bar," I said quickly.

"There is no bar, but I can get you a table," he said just as quickly. "Which show do you want to see, the dinner show or the cocktail show?"

I settled for the cocktail show and was told what time to be there.

Arriving at the appointed time, I was seated promptly and served the first of my two Mai Tai's as the house lights dimmed, and the man was introduced. "And now, for your entertainment, here is Don Ho, singing, 'Tiny Bubbles.'"

I couldn't imagine him opening with his most famous tune, and we gave him a standing ovation as he broke into the familiar refrain, "Tiny bubbles, in the wine…"

After another standing ovation at the end, Don smiled, bowed and said, "I hate that song. I sing a lot better songs than that, but that's the one you folks come to hear, so I like to get it out of the way first so you won't be yelling for it during the rest of the show."

That made sense to me, so I settled back and really enjoyed the rest of the show, and indeed, he did sing a lot better songs. In fact, his show lasted two hours and was very enjoyable, not the tourist trap scene I was really expecting.

Don ended the show by singing, "Tiny Bubbles" again.

After paying the tab, I walked outside just as Don was setting up his "autography party" stool and dais. He was autographing CD's. So I bought a CD that included "Tiny Bubbles" (of course) and walked over and handed it to him, saying, "You've made my night."

"No, sir," he smiled, "you've made *my* night by being here."

I shall never forget that moment. No celebrity had ever said that to me before.

Paul Harvey, in announcing Don's death on his radio news program, said it best: "Paradise will never be the same."

Chapter 28
"Oldies"

On May 17, 2008, I journeyed to Meridian, Mississippi to a get-together hosted by my old girlfriend, Cissy. She had gathered some of her friends and classmates together for a rock 'n roll reunion of The Coasters, The Marvellettes, and The Platters, three great groups of the 50's. Cissy and her husband Jim welcomed us to their fashionable home and then led the procession to the site of the concert, a renovated 1800-era opera house, now known as Mississippi State University's Riley Center.

The evening was a gala event, featuring a packed house of kids of the '50's, reliving the good old days. The Coasters led off the entertainment and had us eating out of the palms of their hands with their favorites, including Charlie Brown, "Yaketty Yak" (Don't Talk Back), etc. The Marvellettes followed with their favorites, including, "Please, Mr. Postman."

And then came The Platters who began their set with what I consider their greatest number, "Only You." Hit after hit followed, until they finally concluded the night with what they called their top-selling record of all time, "You've Got the Magic Touch."

Following the concert, Cissy made her way through the crowd over to me and asked, "Do you want to get some autographs?"

"I don't want to hold anybody up," I replied, thinking how sweet it was of her to remember my penchant for collecting the signatures of the stars.

"That's all right," she smiled. "I'll wait for you."

With that assurance, I made my way to the area where The Platters and The Coasters had set up tables and were signing their CD's. I sidled up to the tables and bought a CD from each group. While getting them to sign, I learned that there was only one original member left in one of the groups. I made sure I got his signature and also shook his hand.

I left the musicians that night thinking, "This might be the last time I have to opportunity to thank this guy for all the moments of great entertainment he provided for me and my friends over the years."

Chapter 29
"n Goodies"

Have you ever looked at the cover of a John Grisham book? Have you ever taken a close look at the picture of the author? That smirk has always painted him, in my eyes, as a cocky smartass.

Until I met him, that is.

Actually, he's a cool dude.

In February of 2008, I had the opportunity to attend a press conference with my friend, Boo Ferriss, in connection with Grisham's appearance at Delta State University, an event appropriately titled, "Books, Baseball, and Boo."

Grisham entered the Boo Ferriss Museum first, confident and casually dressed. He sat down, crossed his legs, and briefly outlined his career, not revealing the sense of humor he would exhibit later that evening at the formal portion of the event. He skirted his baseball career, which was short, and opened it up for questions.

No braggadocio at all. Just the facts. He was brief in answering questions, exhibiting no hint of a sense of humor. As he was departing to make room for Boo to face the media, he moved toward a side door, and I hastened to cut him off.

"Would you please sign my autograph book?" I asked hopefully.

Since the event was scheduled to be a fundraiser for the Delta State athletic program, I figured Grisham would put a price on his signature during the day. To my pleasant surprise, he didn't.

"Certainly," he smiled. Grabbing my book, he signed simply, "John Grisham: and then at the bottom, penned the date (2/11/08) and location (DSU) of the signing. I didn't have the time to ask him if he dated every signature, as he handed the book back to me with a smile and hurried out the door.

That evening, Grisham was a stand-up comedian. He related his short term as a walk-on member of Boo's baseball team in 1974. His narrative of his last intra-squad game had the audience howling. His wit was dry and was delivered with timing that Bob Hope and Jack Benny would have envied, to say nothing of Johnny Carson.

Grisham stood humbly when Delta State bestowed a game jersey and cap upon him. He even outbid those in attendance for the autographed jersey of the pitcher who struck him out during his 1974 intra-squad appearance. He bid $1,500 to win the jersey.

Grisham also offered the top bidder of the evening the opportunity to have his or her name as a character in his next book. He quipped, "I reserve the right to assign your name to the character of my choosing," meaning the character could be killed off on page one, or might appear as the lead character. That opportunity went for $15,000.

SIGN, PLEASE!

All in all, the event raised over $100,000 for the Delta State athletic program.

When "A Time to Kill" was published, Grisham sent Boo a copy with this inscription: "Thanks for changing my career." He has since sent Boo the same message in all of his books.

My editor's first cousin was a court reporter in North Mississippi when John Grisham first opened his law firm and thinks of John as 'a smart and witty guy.' He's been kind enough to personalize inscriptions in his books for Norma, too.

Yep, John Grisham is a cool dude....who remembers where he came from....and those he met along the way.

Chapter 30
"Unsigned Heroes"

During my time as Managing Editor of the *Clarksdale Press Register* and in my position as Public Information Officer for Tunica County, Mississippi, there are other stories of celebrity contacts in my repertoire, not all of which included autographs.

There is the photographic record of the walk through town with President Bill Clinton on a sweltering July day he spent in Clarksdale in 1999, a day when hundreds of us shook his hands in town and on the rope line at the airport before he got back on his chopper, leaving us feeling more empowered than before he came.

There is the autographed picture of Juice Newton I got after her concert at the Horseshoe Casino's Bluesville. I also was awarded one of Juice's signed guitar picks, which I will treasure forever.

Another star I saw perform at Bluesville and whose autograph I didn't stand in a long line for was Olivia Newton-

SIGN, PLEASE!

John. This is proof that I am, indeed, getting old, as I've been an admirer of Olivia for many years.

Then there's the autographed picture of Marcia Ball, a blues pianist who can hang in there with the great pianists of the world and who I first saw at the Jazz and Heritage Festival in New Orleans. I have since caught her act at the Blues Stage in Clarksdale as well as at Ground Zero, the Clarksdale blues club co-owned by Academy Award winning actor Morgan Freeman and local attorney and gubernatorial candidate, Bill Luckett.

John Payne, a noted actor of his time, gave me an autograph while promoting one of his pictures at the Don Theater in Shreveport. He didn't look like he was having any fun, as I recall, but I still have his signature.

In 1976, I took Martha and Stephanie to Hollywood where we took the VIP tour of Universal Studios. Our tram passed stars Victoria Principal and Henry Winkler, immensely popular as "The Fonz" on the incredibly successful show, "Happy Days."

Later, on the same studio tour, we got to see the trailer occupied by one of my favorite actors, Robert Blake. Blake had gotten my attention playing Perry Smith, one of the killers of the Clutter family in the movie portrayal of Truman Capote's book, "In Cold Blood." I certainly didn't want him mad at me, even if it cost me a chance at an autograph. We were assured he was inside the trailer, sleeping, and were warned not to wake him up because he had a temper. So, quiet as church mice we were.

Once, on a flight to San Antonio, I spotted the beautiful Lauren Bacall, longtime wife of actor Humphrey Bogart. Although in her 60's, she was still a beautiful woman, and her voice was still unmistakable. I thanked her for what she had done for Bogie during his illness, and she smiled and said, simply, "Thank you, very much."

Of course, as I have said, when I was with the Saints, I had the opportunity to meet a lot of "stars" when it wasn't kosher to ask for an autograph. One notable that I didn't get was O. J. Simpson. I was visiting when O. J. just walked into the office of the Director of PR for the Buffalo Bills and I was introduced to him. For some reason, I didn't ask O. J. for his autograph.

Others I met in the course of my work include Don Shula, coach of the Miami Dolphins, Al Davis, general manager of the Oakland Raiders, John Robinson, coach of the Los Angeles Rams, Yogi Berra, all-star catcher for the New York Yankees, Lee Majors, the 'Six-Million Dollar Man,' and A. J. Foyt, four-time winner of the Indianapolis 500.

There was also Kay Star, the vixen singer who was a personal friend of John Mecom. She was at one of the parties I was invited to, just sitting on the couch enjoying the party like the rest of us, having a good time.

When one of "Charlie's Angels," Kate Jackson, was a student at Ole Miss, I wanted her to represent Ole Miss in the Miss SEC competition, until I saw Karen Cope, who did compete, and who won!

Finally, there have been times when I just didn't want to fight the large crowd skirmishing for position for an autograph. Celebrities in this category include Willie Nelson, the Beach Boys, and the Oak Ridge Boys.

I've seen and met 'em all and consider myself lucky to have done so.

Very lucky, indeed.

"Braggin' Page"

Larry is past president of the Robinsonville MS Rotary Club, of Clarksdale MS Kiwanis Club, and of the Regional and Mississippi chapters of the "Friends of the Med," home of the Elvis Presley Trauma Center in Memphis. He serves as First Vice-Commander of the Cooper-Yerger American Legion Post 28 in Clarksdale.

He is First Vice-President of the NACIO National Association of County Information Officers, slated to preside as NCAIO President in July of.2011.He has served as Director of PR for Children's Hospital of New Orleans and Director of Marketing for Slidell LA Memorial Hospital.

Larry was Sportswriter and later Managing Editor of the Clarksdale MS Press Register. His column "Liddell's Inkwell" has appeared in The Clarksdale Press Register, The Cleveland News Leader, and the Clarksdale Blues-Star newspapers and currently appears in the monthly "Q" Magazine in Quitman County MS.

He was Director of Public Relations for the New Orleans Saints NFL football team for six years.

As Public Information Officer for Tunica County MS, Larry is often seen on Memphis TV stations, reporting on events from the nine casinos and resort hotels, Tunica National Golf Course, the Olympic Aquatic and Expo Centers, and numerous Mississippi Delta festivals held in the county.

In the winter of 2011, Larry was honored by the All-American Football Foundation with the Fred Russell Lifetime Sportwriting Award. He and his wife Martha, a "Teacher of the Year," live in Clarksdale, Mississippi

Would you like to see your manuscript become a book?

If you are interested in becoming a PublishAmerica author, please submit your manuscript for possible publication to us at:

acquisitions@publishamerica.com

You may also mail in your manuscript to:

**PublishAmerica
PO Box 151
Frederick, MD 21705**

www.publishamerica.com

PublishAmerica